I0759486

Daily Strength for Girls
BroadStreet
KIDS

BroadStreet Publishing Group, LLC.
Savage, Minnesota, USA
Broadstreetpublishing.com

Daily Strength for Girls

9781424569830
9781424569847 eBook

Devotional entries compiled by Jeanna Harder.

Typesetting and design by Garborg Design Works | garborgdesign.com
Editorial services by Michelle Winger | literallyprecise.com

Printed in China.

25 26 27 28 29 30 31 7 6 5 4 3 2 1

The people who trust the Lord
will become strong again.
They will be able to rise up
as an eagle in the sky.
They will run
without needing rest.
They will walk
without becoming tired
Isaiah 40:31 ICB

Introduction

Daily Strength for Girls is a daily devotional book that helps girls like you discover your God-given value, know his love, and depend on him for everything you need.

In this book, you will find

- devotions that encourage you to live boldly and faithfully,
- powerful Bible verses that show God's perfect love and hope-filled promises, and
- simple prayers that help you talk with God.

From dealing with difficult things to being kind and courageous, *Daily Strength for Girls* will give you tools for growing up with a strong, faith-filled heart.

JANUARY
God is our protection and our strength.
He always helps in times of trouble.
Psalm 46:1 ICB

Puzzle Pieces

No one can explain the things God decides. No one can understand God's ways.

ROMANS 11:33 ICB

Imagine puzzle pieces scattered across a table—yellow, pink, brown, and purple pieces. Somehow, they all fit into a picture of four cupcakes covered with colorful frosting. Each piece needs to fit together in order to create the picture on the box.

Every day of your life is like a puzzle piece. Sometimes things happen that don't make sense, but you can be sure God knows. He sees everything. He has a beautiful picture to show you someday when all the pieces of your life fit together.

Dear God, help me to trust that you have an amazing plan for all the pieces of my life.

All Talk

All hard work pays off.
But if all you do is talk, you will be poor.

PROVERBS 14:23 NIRV

Mom pulled out a pan of freshly baked cookies from the oven and put them on a plate to cool.

"I wish I could bake," said Morgan as she bit into a warm chocolate chip cookie.

"You could learn. I could teach you," Mom said as she scooped cookie dough balls onto the baking sheet.

You can wish or talk about what you want to do, or you can make a plan and do it. What do you want to learn to do? Bake cookies, play piano, do a cartwheel, speak Spanish? Go for it!

Dear God, instead of just dreaming, give me the courage to take steps to do the things I want to do.

A Real Princess

"I will be your father,and you will be my sons and daughters."

2 CORINTHIANS 6:18 ICB

Wouldn't it be cool to be a princess, even if just for one day? To be driven around in a golden coach pulled by a team of white horses and wear big dresses and diamonds. As the princess, you are important enough to get to talk to the king—your father.

If you've asked Jesus into your heart, then you are the daughter of the King. He has adopted you into his family and called you his own. You don't live in a castle or wear a crown, but you are deeply loved by the King of the whole universe.

Dear God, thank you for adopting me into your family and calling me your daughter.

A Case of the Giggles

A cheerful heart makes you healthy.
But a broken spirit dries you up.

PROVERBS 17:22 NIRV

Have you ever been somewhere and had a giggle that you couldn't keep inside? Maybe a friend made you laugh. Did you know that giggles can spread from one person to another until pretty soon other people are laughing too.

Getting someone to laugh can make them feel better. If you know someone is unhappy, you can try to make them smile. Sometimes just smiling is the best place to start.

Dear God, I'm glad you gave us giggles and laughter. Help me cheer others up by making them smile.

JANUARY 5

Safe Sleep

In peace I will lie down and sleep.
LORD, you alone keep me safe.

PSALM 4:8 NIRV

Some days can feel so long! Maybe you have to wake up early to eat breakfast and feed the dog before you catch the bus. After school you might have piano lessons or sports practice. Then you go home for dinner, do your homework, take a shower, and read your Bible before bed. That is a full day!

Before you close your eyes and drift off to sleep, take a minute to remember that the Lord watches over you and your family. You can sleep peacefully because you know you are safe.

Dear God, thank you that wherever I am and wherever I go, you're always watching over me.

Being Bold

Be on your guard. Remain strong in the faith. Be brave.
Be loving in everything you do.

1 Corinthians 16:13-14 NIrV

If you have gone hiking on a dirt trail, you may have come across animal paw prints. You may have even seen some wild animals in the woods. That can be scary!

Everyone has things they are afraid of. What kinds of fears do you have? You can ask God to make you bold. You can practice having courage. The Bible says to be on guard. That's like having a good plan in case friends try to get you to do something wrong. Ask the Lord to make you strong and stand up for what is right.

Dear Lord, I don't always feel bold, but I want to be.
Give me courage to say no to bad ideas.

His Voice

Whether you turn to the right or to the left, your ears will hear a voice behind you, saying, "This is the way; walk in it."

ISAIAH 30:21 NIV

You have heard your mom's voice so often that you'd recognize it right away on the phone or in a crowd of people talking. You've heard it since you were a baby. God promises to speak to the people who follow him. He can speak to you and guide you.

How do you learn to know God's voice? Believe in Jesus. Read his words in the Bible. God loves to speak, and he loves it even more when you listen. Ask him to speak to you right now.

Dear God, thank you for speaking to me in different ways. Help me recognize your voice and listen to you.

Write It Down

I remember what the LORD did;
I remember the miracles you did long ago.

PSALM 77:11 NCV

Your mom may have had a journal that she wrote her feelings in or recorded special things that happened to her. Writing things down helps you express your feelings and remember important events.

You can read back through your journal and remember the good things God did and see how he answered your prayers. Remember who God is and thank him for being such a good God.

Dear God, I remember when you answered my prayer. Thank you for being so good to me.

Name Change

You were taught to be made new in your hearts, to become a new person. That new person is made to be like God—made to be truly good and holy.

EPHESIANS 4:23-24 NCV

Do you remember learning about the Saul in the Bible? Saul was smart, powerful, and mean! He made fun of Christians, and even hurt them. One day, while he was riding to another city, God completely changed his life. He even changed his name from Saul to Paul. Paul became a Christian and spent the rest of his life telling people how to live for Jesus. He was a new person.

You may know kids who are mean and rude. You might feel like avoiding them. But remember that God can change people like he changed Saul.

Dear God, remind me to pray for the kids who are mean. Show me what I can say or do to help them.

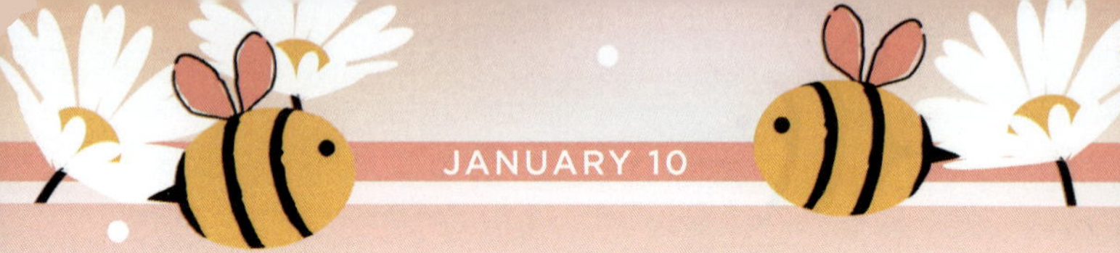

A Good Name

Never let loyalty and kindness leave you!
Write them deep within your heart.
Then you will find favor with both God and people,
and you will earn a good reputation.

PROVERBS 3:3-4 NLT

Famous people get a lot of attention. People know their names, what they look like, and even know the number on their jersey if they play sports. But do they have a good reputation?

Loyalty and kindness, rather than money and fame, gives people a good name, not just with people but with God. Being loyal and kind is something everyone can do.

Dear God, I want to be a good person, so when someone says my name, they think good things.

JANUARY 11

"Whoever can be trusted with a little can also be trusted with a lot, and whoever is dishonest with a little is dishonest with a lot."

LUKE 16:10 NCV

Some people are unreliable. You don't know if you can trust them to do what they say they will do. You ask them to do something, and they don't. They promise they'll give you something and they don't. You ask them to keep a secret, but you find out they told someone. You quickly learn you cannot trust them.

Being the kind of person people can count on is important. Your parents will give you more important things when you show them that you can take care of little things.

Dear God, help me to be someone that other people can count on.

JANUARY 12

No Limitations

With God's power working in us, God can do much, much more than anything we can ask or imagine.

EPHESIANS 3:20 NCV

Some people have disabilities, and their bodies or brains don't work the same as other people's. There are limits to what a disabled person can do, but God doesn't see their limitations as something wrong. He has a special plan for each person.

Nothing can stand in the way of God using anyone for his good plan. Nothing can limit God. God uses young kids and old people. He uses happy and sad people. He uses able-bodied people and disabled people. God can use anyone, anywhere, anytime to do anything!

Dear God, you are so powerful that there is nothing you can't do!

It's Not Ok

"I hold you by your right hand—
I, the Lord your God.
And I say to you,
'Don't be afraid. I am here to help you.'"

Isaiah 41:13 NLT

There are some things you can put up with, like being teased by your dad or your best friend. Some things are funny, but there are other things that aren't. Being bullied is not okay. It's important to stand up for yourself and others who are hurting. If you need help, ask an adult you trust.

Tell God how you're feeling. Then pray for the people who are being unkind. They might be hurting too. Ask God what to do and listen to what he says. He answers prayers.

Dear God, sometimes it's hard to stand up for myself. Please give me wisdom and strength.

A Grump

We who are strong in faith should help those who are weak. We should help them with their weaknessess, and not please only ourselves.

ROMANS 15:1 ICB

Naomi was a woman in the Bible who had a lot of sad things happen to her. She became a grumpy lady and told people to call her bitter. So many things went wrong in her life that she thought God had forgot about her, but God put Ruth in her life.

Ruth stuck with Naomi even though she was grumpy and wasn't fun to be around. Ruth was kind and loyal. God used Ruth to help change Naomi's sad heart. God can use you to help change someone's heart too.

Dear God, when I'm around someone grumpy, show me how to show them love.

A Bad Taste

Do everything without complaining and arguing, so that no one can criticize you. Live clean, innocent lives as children of God, shining like bright lights.

PHILIPPIANS 2:14-15 NLT

Have you taken a bite of food that tasted bad? Yuck! A bad taste in your mouth is awful. Complaining is like that. It doesn't fix things, and it is not pleasant to listen to.

As a child of God, complaining doesn't belong in your mouth. You are supposed to shine like a bright light that helps people see who God is. He is loving and caring, and you should be, too. Let people hear thankful, kind, honest words come out of your mouth.

Dear God, I don't want to be a complainer.
Help me to shine bright for you.

My Shepherd

The LORD is my shepherd;
I have everything I need.

PSALM 23:1 NCV

A shepherd takes care of his sheep. He will fight off other animals that try to hurt the sheep. He leads them to water and new green pastures to eat. He bandages their wounds and will go looking for them if they wander away or get lost.

The Lord is your shepherd. He can provide for your needs. He will lead you if you follow him. He keeps you safe. He can heal you. You are never too far away that he won't find you. He loves watching over you.

Dear Lord, you are my shepherd.
I have everything I need in you.

JANUARY 17

Family First

"Honor your father and mother."

EXODUS 20:12 NIRV

Your parents probably ask you how your day was or if you finished your homework. They probably also remind you to do important things. They say these sorts of things because they care about you.

God is a father to the fatherless. He helps those who don't have parents anymore. God sometimes uses his people to help him take care of them. You are part of God's plan because you are part of his family.

Dear God, thank you for making me a part of your family. Show me how I can help take care of others.

They Matter

Dear friends, if God loved us in this way, we also must love one another.

1 John 4:11 CSB

God loves you and cares about each detail of your life. That's true for you and for those around you—your younger brother or sister, little cousins, or neighbor kids. If God cares about them, you should too.

Little kids need to be shown love in a way they can understand. Listen to them even if you've heard them say the same thing before. Look at them even if you see something else more interesting. Spend time with them even if you'd rather be doing something else. That's how Jesus loves you.

Dear Lord, thank you for being a good example of what loving others looks like.

A Book of Letters

My child, listen to your father's teaching
and do not forget your mother's advice.

PROVERBS 1:8 NCV

Some of the books of the Bible record important events in history. Some list families. Some offer a lot of good advice or warnings and consequences of bad choices. The Bible is a roadmap to living a good life. You can trust that everything written in it is true.

Your mom or dad also give you advice. They are the ones who care about you the most. When they tell you to do something, it is to help you, teach you, and protect you. Listening to them will help make your life better, and you won't regret it.

Dear God, thank you for caring parents who give me helpful advice. Help me learn from them.

JANUARY 20

R-E-S-P-E-C-T

Show proper respect to everyone. Love the family of believers. Have respect for God. Honor the emperor.

1 PETER 2:17 NIRV

Peanut butter and jelly, pen and paper, socks and shoes. Some things just naturally go together. They come in pairs. If you say one word, you think the other. The same is true of respect. What are some things that go well with respect? Listening, politeness, caring.

You don't have to agree with everyone all the time. You can disagree and still show respect. Being respectful is something important you need to learn. It will help you become more like Jesus.

Dear God, I know how I treat people is important because people are important to you.

Quick and Slow

Everyone should be quick to listen, slow to speak and slow to become angry.

JAMES 1:19 NIV

It always seems like a good thing to be fast. Fast food. Fast Wi-Fi. You might be a fast runner or fast at math. Being slow isn't usually seen as a good thing. No one wants to be the last one to do anything.

What about when it comes to anger though? Do you get mad easily? Are you quick to talk back? God says you should be slow to get angry instead of reacting too quickly when you are mad. This helps you avoid saying the wrong thing and hurting others.

Dear God, teach me to stop, wait, listen, and then respond in the right way.

Horse Sense

Don't be like a horse or a mule.
They can't understand anything.
They have to be controlled by bits and bridles.
If they aren't, they won't come to you.

PSALM 32:9 NIRV

Have you gone on a horseback ride? Once you are up in the saddle, you use the reins to steer the horse along the path. Horseback riding can be a lot of fun, but it can also be frustrating and even scary if the horse doesn't obey you and goes whichever way it wants to go.

Sometimes we have our own ideas about what we should do. Maybe you don't feel like doing what God says, or it doesn't make sense to you, or everyone else is doing something different. Don't miss out on God's goodness. Do what you know is best—follow his ways.

Dear God, you are the best leader. Help me to follow you and not myself or others.

Search and Find

"You will search for me. And when you search for me with all your heart, you will find me!"

JEREMIAH 29:13 ICB

When something is lost, it can send you on a wild goose chase looking for it. You will search everywhere! You probably look under your bed, pull out the couch cushions, dump out your backpack, empty drawers, and ask someone else to help you search.

Looking for God isn't nearly as hard as looking for something like that. God isn't hiding. He wants to spend time with you and help you understand him.

Dear God, you have all the answers.
Thank you for always being with me.

JANUARY 24

Worth It

The lazy will not get what they want,
but those who work hard will.

Proverbs 13:4 NCV

What do you dream about doing? Becoming a goal-scoring soccer player, winning the spelling bee, playing the grand finale at a concert? If you have a goal to get first place, you must work hard each day.

To reach your goals, you need to work for it and not make excuses or be lazy. You have to put in the work. Many times, the difference between those who succeed and those who don't is just plain old hard work.

Dear God, instead of feeling discouraged or lazy,
help me to focus on my goal.

Live by Truth

I see your love,
and I live by your truth.
PSALM 26:3 NCV

What pushes you to do the best you can? Does a reward at the end motivate you to complete a task? God knew that we needed rewards, so he built them into things he asks us to do.

Telling the truth isn't just something you're supposed to do; it's something that comes with a reward for you. You will earn trust people's trust, and you won't feel guilty for lying.

Dear God, help me to see the rewards you built into being truthful.

Elephant in the Room

He stores up wisdom for those who are honest.
Like a shield he protects the innocent.
PROVERBS 2:7 NCV

What if there really were an elephant in your room? You'd have to walk around the elephant to get to the closet, or under the elephant to get to your bed, or over it to reach your dresser. Or maybe your room is so small you could only squeeze a baby elephant inside.

Some families argue when there's a problem. Others hold their feelings inside. Everyone knows there is a problem, but no one wants to talk about it. This is what we call having an elephant in the room. It's awkward. Don't let elephants sit in the room. Work on your problems together.

Dear God, give me wisdom to know how to talk about things that are hard.

Prickly People

"Love your enemies. Pray for those who hurt you."

MATTHEW 5:44 NCV

Thistles are tall prickly weeds topped with a bright purple flower. They can quickly take over a garden. Touching them or stepping on them hurts. Some people can be like thistles: prickly, crabby, and hurtful. Their bad mood spreads to those around them.

Underneath that prickly surface is a person God loves. He understands why they seem crabby. He sees their hurting hearts and the pain they feel. He cares for them. Do you know someone who's seems prickly? Maybe God will use you to help them feel loved.

Dear God, help me to see people like you see them. Remind me to show them love.

Great at Serving

"Whoever wants to become great among you must be your servant."

MARK 10:43 NIV

Do you know girls who have done really great things? Creative thinking, hard work, and perseverance probably brought them success.

In God's kingdom, you are great if you serve others. You can clear dirty dishes from the table, empty the dishwasher, or take out the trash without being asked. Hold the door open for the person behind you. Volunteer at church or in your community. Doing great things doesn't make you great, serving others does.

Dear God, help me to have a heart that wants to serve others.

Over-the-Top

Your love, LORD, reaches to the heavens,
your faithfulness to the skies.

PSALM 36:5 NIV

Guess how far the sky stretches up to heaven. You're right. You can't measure that, just like you can't measure how high and deep and wide God's love is. God's love is amazing, over-the-top, eternal, patient, inclusive, dependable, and powerful.

There's no way to measure God's love; it's that big. His love is big enough for you, your family, your neighbors, your classmates, people all around the world. God's love is a treasure to be shared.

Dear God, your love is amazing!
It's more than I can even try to imagine.

Favorite Things

Find your delight in the LORD.
Then he will give you everything your heart really wants.

PSALM 37:4 NIRV

What is your favorite food? Does your mom or dad know? Would you trust them to order food for you at a restaurant? When someone knows you really well and really loves you, trusting them comes easily. You can trust they know what you like.

You know God really loves you, so you can be sure he'll choose something for you that you like. Instead of worrying about something, spend your energy trusting God.

Dear God, you know me better than anyone else.
I trust you will always choose the best for me.

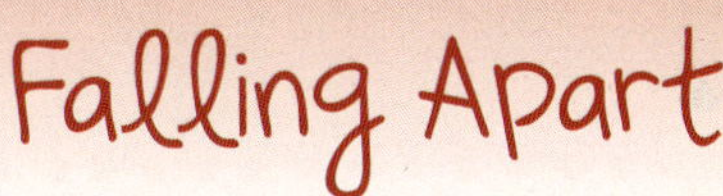

Falling Apart

The Lord shows his true love every day.
At night I have a song,
and I pray to my living God.

PSALM 42:8 ICB

Some parents fight and argue and can work things out. But some parents can't, and they get divorced. When it feels like life is falling apart, God knows. He sees and he cares about what is happening.

Even if families separate, that doesn't separate any of them from God's love. God still has a plan and purpose for each person's life. If you know someone whose family is going through a tough time (or if your family is going through a tough time), pray for God's love to be close.

Dear God, help me to trust that your love never changes.

FEBRUARY
The name of the LORD
is like a strong tower.
Godly people run to it
and are safe.
PROVERBS 18:10 NIRV

Behind the Bragging

I always remember you in my prayers, asking the God of our Lord Jesus Christ, the glorious Father, to give you a spirit of wisdom and revelation so that you will know him better.

EPHESIANS 1:16-17 NCV

When people brag about how smart they are or the cool things they did or have, it can make others feel less important. God made everyone with abilities to do things for his plan.

Some people brag because they are proud of what they've done and want everyone to know. But people also brag to try and feel better about themselves. Maybe they don't really know God or understand that he really loves them. If you come across a person who brags a lot, pray for them.

Dear God, help me to see people the way you see them.

FEBRUARY 2

A Choice

Of all the people on earth, the LORD your God has chosen you to be his own special treasure.

DEUTERONOMY 7:6 NLT

If you had a choice, would you design a clothing line, run the company that made the clothing line, help girls pick clothes that make them look good, or model the new clothes. Some of us are creative, some are leaders, some like to organize, and others like to help people.

You don't need to impress God with how much you know or do. He chooses you because he loves you, not because you've earned it.

Dear God, thank you for choosing me to be in your family. I feel special just knowing that.

A Little While

God always gives you all the grace you need. So you will only have to suffer for a little while. Then God himself will build you up again.

1 PETER 5:10 NIRV

To *suffer* is to experience something painful. Everybody goes through hard times. No one enjoys suffering but remember it won't last forever. Try not to let bad things get you down. Look for the good things you have.

Hard things don't have to stop you from becoming a strong, young lady who loves Jesus and still trusts him no matter what happens. Suffering is for a little while, but being with Jesus is forever!

Dear God, thank you that no matter what happens, I can lean on you.

Where You Go

"Where you go, I will go. Where you live, I will live. Your people will be my people, and your God will be my God."

RUTH 1:16 NCV

Ruth is a famous woman of the Bible. She lived with her mother-in-law, Naomi, who was so sad from losing all of the men in her family that she decided move back to her hometown. Ruth was also sad. That's when she said the Bible verse above.

Ruth was connected to Naomi in a special way because they both believed in the one true God. Do you have a Christian friend who you like to be with? It is good to have friends who share your belief in God and walk with you through the happy and sad times.

Dear Lord, you are my God, and I am thankful that I will always have you in my life.

FEBRUARY 5

"I am going there to prepare a place for you."

JOHN 14:2 NCV

Wouldn't a total bedroom change be a cool surprise? Imagine freshly painted walls in whatever color you want, a new bunkbed, string lights, a giant pillow puff chair, a new bedspread and matching curtains, and cool pictures hanging on the walls. That would be amazing!

Before Jesus rose up into heaven, he said he would go and prepare a place for us. It will be better than the most amazing room you've ever seen. Everything will be new and beautiful! You can read about it in your Bible in Revelation 21 and 22.

Dear Jesus, I'm excited to see the home you're preparing for me.

Valuable Masterpiece

We are God's masterpiece.

Ephesians 2:10 NLT

Name brand shoes, purses, and clothing all have a label that tells you who made it. Some brands are worth more than others. With good brand names, you can trust the item is good quality.

You were made by the Creator of heaven and earth. The Bible says you are his masterpiece. Your worth and value comes from God. It doesn't come from what you have or what you can do. When you feel bad about something about yourself, remember who made you!

Dear God, thank you for making me
a valuable masterpiece.

Feeling Good

God, we come into your Temple.
There we think about your love.

PSALM 48:9 ICB

Think of someone you love to be around. Are they fun, happy, and kind? Does thinking of that person make you smile? Spending time with God does the same thing. Think about who he is, how much he loves you, and how special you are to him.

God is always kind and doesn't get angry quickly. Close your eyes, take a long, slow breath, and think about how much God loves you. Don't forget to smile back at him.

Dear God, I feel good when I spend time with you.
Each day there are more things I can thank you for.

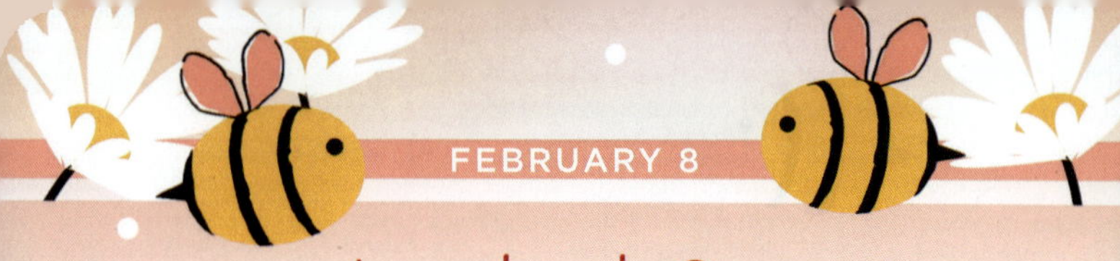

Lost at Sea

I pray that you and all God's holy people will have the power to understand the greatness of Christ's love—how wide and how long and how high and how deep that love is.

EPHESIANS 3:18 NCV

If God's love were an ocean, you'd get lost in its bigness. It stretches wider than the sea and deeper too. It's too great to understand on your own.

You need God to help you understand how high, wide, and deep his love is. Ask him to show you his love, and then look for it each day.

Dear God, show me how wide, deep, and high your love is for me.

Thunderstorms

God is our refuge and strength,
an ever-present help in trouble.

PSALM 46:1 NIV

Thunder boomed and lightning cracked. The wind howled and the house seemed to shake. The trees outside the window were swaying back and forth. Have you even been afraid during a storm? Does it help to sit with your parents? Knowing they are close can make you feel safe.

When bad things happen, you might not think that God is around, but the Bible says he is always close, ready to help. He won't leave you. He will comfort you and fill you with his peace.

Dear God, no matter what happens, thank you for always being there to help me.

Stay Close

The LORD is my place of safety.
Why should I be afraid?

PSALM 27:1 NIRV

Camping trips can be so fun! Days filled with fishing and canoeing, exploring the woods, and setting up camp. At night it gets dark with just the light from the campfire and maybe a flashlight. You need to stick close to whoever has the flashlight if you need to go somewhere.

The same is true with God. When you walk close to him, you can see where you're going and what to do because he is the light. He protects you and shows you where to go. He can help you make good decisions.

Dear God, help me to know not just in my head but my heart that you are near.

Good Fear

If you really want to gain knowledge,
you must begin by having respect for the LORD.
But foolish people hate wisdom and instruction.

PROVERBS 1:7 NIRV

Are you the type of kid who isn't afraid to do things—roller coasters, skiing, skateboarding? How do you feel about spiders, snakes, or mice? What about speaking or singing in front of a large group of people? Last one. Are you ever afraid of getting in trouble with your parents?

Your parents aren't being mean when they give you consequences for poor choices. It's their job. The fear of getting in trouble can keep you from doing wrong. It's a good kind of fear. When you learn to listen to that fear you will become smarter.

Dear God, help me to have a good fear for my parents and for you.

Being the Boss

Remind the believers to do these things: to be under the authority or rulers and government leaders, to obey them and be ready to do good.

TITUS 3:1 ICB

If you have spent time with young children, you know they don't always listen to the person who is in charge of them. It might sound fun to be the person in charge, but it can be tiring. When people don't want to do what you tell them to do, it stops being fun.

Try to support the person who is in charge. You can lead others by being an example. Listen and do what is asked with a good attitude. Being in charge can be hard work, but you can make it easier.

Dear God, remind me to be good to those you have put in charge of me.

Being Great

"Whoever wants to become great among you must be your servant."

MATTHEW 20:26 NIV

There have been girls as young as fifteen who have won gold medals. One girl developed a website idea at age ten that is now worth millions of dollars. These girls accomplished great things at a young age but consider where they started. They had an idea, and they worked hard without giving up until they reached it.

It's different in God's kingdom. Being great means being a servant. It means that you think about others. God is most proud of you when you choose to love and serve others.

Dear God, show me how to be great in your kingdom by serving others.

Love Like That

Continue to love one another, for love comes from God.

1 JOHN 4:7 NLT

People like to be loved differently. Some people like to hear it. Others prefer a hug. Some really appreciate thoughtful gifts. Maybe you like it when someone spends time with you or does something for you.

God not only created love, he is love. He calls you his child, takes care of your needs, and invites you to spend time with him. Maybe he will send someone to give you a hug or help you clean your room. He knows the best way to love you.

Dear God, thank you for loving me in so many ways.

Noticed

"Your Father sees what is done in secret, and he will reward you."

MATTHEW 6:18 NCV

How would you feel if you did something amazing and no one noticed? If you organized your closet and drawers without being asked or came up with a great school fundraiser idea that someone else took credit for, it would be disappointing.

It's nice to be noticed, but people don't always say anything. God notices! He pays attention to what you do and sees the good things others might not. He will reward you. Maybe not right away. Maybe not in the way you expect. But he will reward you!

Dear God, thank you for noticing me.
Thank you for the reward I will receive one day.

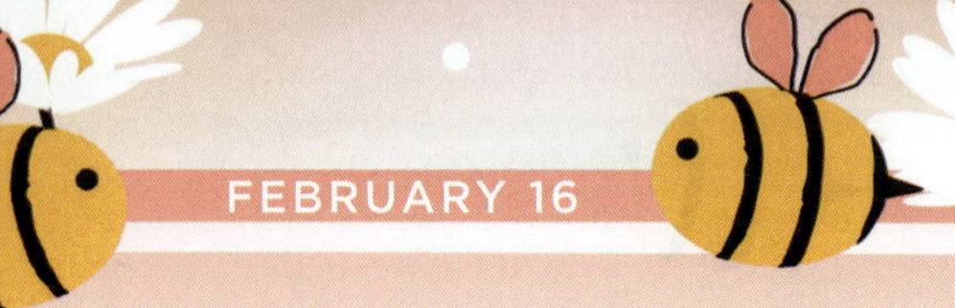

FEBRUARY 16

It Will Cost You

Give me an undivided heart,
that I may fear your name.

PSALM 86:11 NIV

Along the coast, brown pelicans dive headfirst into the ocean and scoop up fish in their large pouch-like beaks. Seagulls will sometimes sit on a pelican's head and distract it by pecking its head, then snatch the fish that drop from the pelican's beak. The seagulls get a free meal, and the poor pelican has lost its dinner.

Distractions can cost you too. If you are distracted, you might miss something important. Distractions can keep you from loving God with all your heart. Pay attention to things that might be taking your attention away from God.

Dear God, teach me to focus on what's important and what needs my full attention.

Growing

We should always thank God for you. That is only right, because your faith is growing more and more.

2 Thessalonians 1:3 NIRV

Are you into horses, art, ballet, soccer, or something else? You will enjoy learning more about something you are interested in. Faith in God is like that. The more you read God's Word and spend time talking to him, the more you understand who he is and what he's done for you.

You can grow your faith in God by singing to him, memorizing Bible verses, talking to him in the morning, and listening for his voice at night.

Dear God, I want my faith to grow.
Show me creative ways to grow in you.

What You Expect

"Have mercy, just as your Father has mercy."

LUKE 6:36 NIRV

When someone doesn't do what you expect or want them to do for you, it makes you wonder if they care about you. The truth might be completely different than what you're thinking.

Think the best of others and don't assume the worst. You can show mercy when things don't go as you hope.

Dear God, show me how to show mercy like you do.

Use Your Imagination

"In everything, do to others what you would want them to do to you"

MATTHEW 7:12 NIRV

Do you like to imagine that you are someone else? Imagine you were a mom, a teacher, or a little kid for a day. How would you want to be treated?

Using your imagination to think about someone else can help you figure out what they might like or not like. Doing to others what you want them to do to you gives you a chance to show them love in a very real way.

Dear God, remind me to think of others,
how they feel and what they need.

Family Night

Children are a gift from the LORD;
they are a reward from him.

PSALM 127:3 NLT

Some families have a special night they call *family night*. They might go on a bike ride, or to a ball game, or to an apple orchard, or roast marshmallows around a bonfire. It is important to make time to be together.

Families are part of God's good plan for us. Do you know that you are one of the most precious gifts your parents have ever been given? The Bible calls children a reward. It may not always feel like it, but you are an important part of your family.

Dear God, thank you for my family.
We're not perfect, but we are better together.

Family Buffet

Accept one another, then, just as Christ accepted you, in order to bring praise to God.

ROMANS 15:7 NIV

It's fun to go through a buffet and choose what you want. Being part of a family isn't like that though. You can't decide who you do and don't want in it, and you can't pick out the things you don't like.

With family, the hard parts, the good parts, and the parts you don't understand all come together. You can't separate them. Write a list of the things you like most about the people in your family. Then thank God for each person.

Dear God, thank you for making my family just the way they are. Help me appreciate each of them.

The Family Name

"All those who stand before others and say they believe in me, I, the Son of Man, will say before the angels of God that they belong to me."

LUKE 12:8 NCV

Your last name tells people what family you belong to. When you believe in Jesus, you become part of his family and belong to him. You take on his name and call yourself a Christian. He calls you his own and writes your name in his book of life. From that point on, what you say and do reflects him.

When you're faithful to the family of God, he'll say in front of all the angels in heaven, "This is my child. She belongs to me."

Dear Jesus, thank you for giving me your family name. I'm so happy I belong to you.

Name Calling

I bow in prayer before the Father from whom every family in heaven and on earth gets its true name.

EPHESIANS 3:14-15 NCV

Have you ever been called names? *Nerd. Loser. Dumb. Ugly.* Mean words hurt and make you feel bad about yourself. You might not have thought those things, but once someone calls you bad names, it can be hard not to believe it.

When you belong to Jesus, he calls you his own. He removes mean names, peels off bad names you've been called, and gives you his good name. He wraps his big, loving arms around you and says you are beautiful, precious, and loved.

Dear God, thank you for removing all the bad names and giving me your great name.

Adopted

After this I looked, and there in front of me was a huge crowd of people… There were so many that no one could count them. They came from every nation, tribe and people.

REVELATION 7:9 NIRV

Some families have adopted children from different countries where the people look different, talk differently, and might even act differently. Once a child is adopted, he or she is a part of their new family. The differences don't matter.

God has adopted people from every country, tribe, and language. Heaven's streets will be filled with different people! There are people all over the world who love and follow God. What makes us family is who we belong to.

Dear God, remind me to pray for the people in my great big God family.

Special Attention

You are making some people more important than others, and with evil thoughts you are deciding that one person is better.

James 2:4 NCV

This verse is a reminder not to treat people better or worse based on what they look like. Sometimes you get treated better when you are dressed up. People think you have more money or are more important. But that's not true.

You don't know someone's story just by how they look on the outside. Treat everyone with the same level of kindness no matter what they look like.

Dear God, help me treat everyone as important and special because they are to you.

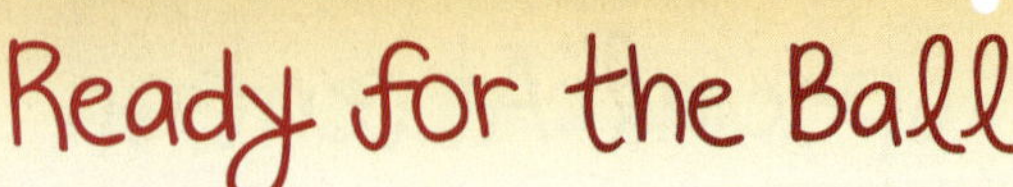

Ready for the Ball

Since God chose you to be the holy people he loves, you must clothe yourselves with tenderhearted mercy, kindness, humility, gentleness and patience.

COLOSSIANS 3:12 NLT

Do you like wearing dresses? It can be fun to get all dressed up and look fancy for special occasions and twirl around in front of the mirror with layers of soft, silky fabric swishing around you.

As you pick out your clothes each day, don't forget to also put on a tender heart, kindness, mercy, humility, gentleness, and patience. These are the most beautiful things to put on.

Dear Lord, when I get dressed every morning, remind me to put on what you consider beautiful.

A New Life

Anyone who belongs to Christ has become a new person.
The old life is gone; a new life has begun!

2 CORINTHIANS 5:17 NLT

New babies are small and sweet. They have soft skin, tiny fingers, and cute little noses. Babies are a reminder of new beginnings.

Jesus said that if you believe in him, he promises to take away everything you've ever done wrong and give you new life. With that new life comes a new beginning. You can start over fresh and new!

Dear Jesus, thank you for the new life you have given me.

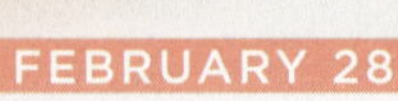

You Can Do It

Let's not get tired of doing what is good. At just the right time we will reap a harvest of blessing if we don't give up.

GALATIANS 6:9 NLT

You may have heard people say you can do anything if you set your mind to it. Well, that's not totally true, but you can do what God created you to do! It takes work and practice and determination.

Doing what is right is hard when you don't feel like it, or when no one else is doing it, or when people make fun of you. The reward, though, is always worth the work. Don't give up. Go for it!

Dear God, help me to remember the reward you promise when I don't give up.

MARCH

The Lord gives strength
to those who are tired.
He gives more power
to those who are weak.

Isaiah 40:29 ICB

Big Bully

What should we say about this? If God is for us, no one can defeat us.

ROMANS 8:31 NCV

Have you had to stand up to a bully? Goliath was a bully to the people of Israel. He made fun of them. And no one dared take him on. Everyone, even the king, was afraid of Goliath. Until David came along.

David had not forgotten that God stands up for his people. With a sling and five smooth stones, David took care of the giant bully. Nobody messes with God's people without him noticing. He always sees what is happening and he will win in the end.

Dear God, it makes me feel so good knowing that you are fighting for me.

Don't Run Away

She gave this name to the LORD who spoke to her: "You are the God who sees me."

GENESIS 16:13 NIV

Sometimes life is hard, and you might want to run away. A woman in the Bible named Hagar felt that way. She ran away from a difficult family situation. But God saw her and knew all about what she was running from.

God knows everything and sees everyone. Nothing and no one miss his attention. Is there something in your life you wish would change? What would you like God to do about it? Talk to him.

Dear God, you know all things, and you care deeply about me.

No Job too Small

See how very much our Father loves us, for he calls us his children, and that is what we are!

1 JOHN 3:1 NLT

There once was a servant girl in the household of a very powerful master. When she found out her master was sick, she knew God could heal him. She told her mistress, and her mistress told her master, and her master went to God's prophet and was healed.

You might think the tasks you have are small and unimportant. Just because you are a young girl doesn't mean God won't or can't use you to do great things!

Dear God, I am young, but I know you can use me to do something important.

You Make God Smile

Without faith no one can please God. Anyone who comes to God must believe that he is real and that he rewards those who truly want to find him.

HEBREWS 11:6 ICB

God likes when you notice him. He loves it when you talk to him like a real person and listen to what he says. Having faith like that puts a smile on God's face.

Believing God will give you courage or show you how to be kind makes God happy. Pouring out your heart to God on a bad day makes him happy too. It shows that you believe he is who he says he is.

Dear God, I believe you are a powerful, loving God who wants to spend time with me.

Snuggles Needed

The LORD is close to all who call on him,
yes, to all who call on him in truth.

PSALM 145:18 NLT

Whether you're a two-year-old or a twelve-year-old, sometimes you just want to snuggle—with your mom or dad, grandma or grandpa, or even your pet. Being close to someone you love makes you feel good, special, and safe.

The Lord is always near. Whether you're feeling excited, scared, sick, or lonely, he is there for you. His loving presence surrounds you with peace and comfort.

Dear God, I just need to know you're close and that you care. Thanks for answering when I call.

A Soft Spot

When the Lord saw her, his heart overflowed with compassion. "Don't cry!" he said.

LUKE 7:13 NLT

Some people have a soft spot for little kids. No matter what the child asks, they just can't say no. Jesus had a soft spot for poor people who were often sad and alone.

If you're a follower of Jesus, you should also show compassion to people who need help. Think of some ways you could show love for the people around you.

Dear God, I want to show love and compassion to people who need to know someone cares.

MARCH 7

A Unique Whistle

"They follow him because they know his voice. But they will never follow a stranger."

JOHN 10:4 NCV

Dolphins talk through clicks, whistles, and squeals. A mother dolphin begins using her special whistle when a baby dolphin is born. The baby will learn to recognize the mother's whistle, so it can find its way back if it gets separated from her.

Learning to recognize God's voice is important, like knowing your parents' voices. You've got to know the difference between what's true and what's not. Don't listen to voices that don't belong to God.

Dear Lord, help me practice listening to your voice so that I will recognize it.

The Good News

"Go into all the world and preach the Good News to everyone."

MARK 16:15 NLT

There are many different ways to share God's good news with people. You could help teach little kids at church. You could become a teacher, or an author, or a singer, or a coach.

You can tell people about God in lots of different ways. Be creative and figure out how you can share the love of Jesus with others.

Dear God, I want to share the good news of Jesus with the people around me.

Smart and Kind

"May you be blessed for your wisdom. You have kept me from killing or punishing people today."

1 SAMUEL 25:33 ICB

Abigail was married to a man named Nabal who was mean and foolish. He was so rude to some messengers that their leader was furious and threatened to kill Nabal and his whole family. Abigail was really smart. She brought gifts to the angry leader and spoke kindly. Because of her quick thinking, the leader changed his mind.

When you stay calm, use wisdom and come up with a positive solution, you can change a bad situation into a good one.

Dear God, give me wisdom to do what is right and help me be a good influence on others.

MARCH 10

Accepted

Your salvation doesn't come from anything you do. It is God's gift. It is not based on anything you have done.

EPHESIANS 2:8-9 NIRV

God accepts you into his family. He loves you even if you don't think you are good enough. God knows you aren't perfect. He doesn't expect you to be.

You can't earn God's love. He accepts you because he loves you and because you believe in him.

Dear God, thank you for accepting me right where I am at. I am not perfect.

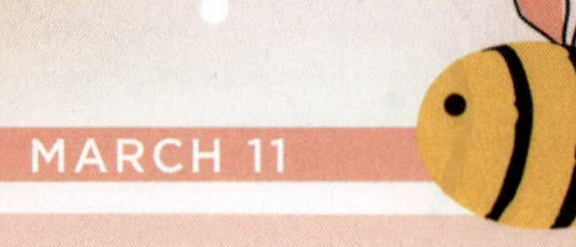

Around the World

Through everything God made, they can clearly see his invisible qualities—his eternal power and divine nature. So they have no excuse for not knowing God.

ROMANS 1:20 NLT

No matter where you are in the world, you can look up and see the same big sky and the same bright sun or moon. All of nature from the sky to the ocean and every living thing on earth are proof that God is real.

Nature also shows God's power. Everyone everywhere can see God through his amazing creation. There is no excuse for not believing in him.

Dear God, you are so great! Thank you for showing everyone everywhere that you are real.

Adventure Awaits

You will fill me with joy in your presence.

PSALM 16:11 NIV

What would an exciting adventure look like to you? Riding a chestnut brown horse, galloping across a grassy field, surrounded by mountains in Montana? Surfing a wave on the bright blue waters of the ocean in Hawaii? Trying to find a secret staircase in an old castle in France?

You're on an adventure every day called *life*. God has packed it with freedom, interesting people and places, and pure joy. Explore and enjoy what God has for you.

Dear God, I'm looking forward to my life adventures with you!

MARCH 13

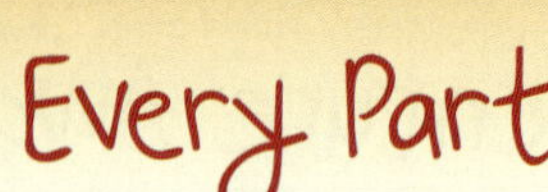

You know the message God sent to the people of Israel. It is the good news of peace through Jesus Christ. He is Lord of all.

ACTS 10:36 NIRV

Imagine a delicious ice cream cake with drizzles of caramel and chocolate on top. Yum! If it were for a birthday, you wouldn't cut out a piece and eat it before the party no matter how much you wanted to take a bite.

Some people try to give their lives to God with missing pieces. They keep part for themselves and give the rest to God. But when you give your life to Jesus, he should be the Lord of everything.

Dear God, I want you to be Lord of all of my life.

Wrap Up and Rest

I find rest in God;
only he can save me.
PSALM 62:1 NCV

There's nothing like a cup of hot chocolate to help warm you up when you're cold. It feels so good to plop down in front of a cozy fire, wrapped in a blanket while you sip warm, chocolatey goodness. You can feel your frozen body start to relax.

Sometimes your insides need to relax from being tired or upset. God wants to be your source of rest. He can help make you feel much better.

Dear God, help me remember to go to you for peace and rest when my heart and mind are bothered.

Welcome

Keep on loving each another as brothers and sisters. Don't forget to show hospitality to strangers.

HEBREWS 13:1-2 NLT

You have probably met someone who moved from another country. They might look different, sound different, and eat different food. They probably feel different too. Treating people with hospitality means making them feel like they belong.

Think of how you can practice hospitality. Help them feel comfortable, and soon they will feel like they are part of the group.

Dear God, show me how I can make someone feel welcome and at home.

MARCH 16

Be very careful how you live. Do not live like those who are not wise, but live wisely.

EPHESIANS 5:15 NCV

People make poor choices with what they say and how they act. The Bible is very clear. When you become a Christian, you are following Jesus and should try your best to act like him.

Jesus has an amazing plan for your life. Listen to the good advice in the verse above. Be very careful how you live and be wise. Your life is a special gift from God.

Dear God, your plans for my life are so good.
Thank you for helping me to live like Jesus.

MARCH 17

Anywhere and Everywhere

I can never escape from your Spirit!
I can never get away from your presence!

PSALM 139:7 NLT

Do you have a favorite spot to get away and talk to God? There's nowhere you can go where he wouldn't be. Everywhere you go, God will be there with you.

You can meet God going on a bike ride, soaking in a bubble bath, or swinging in a hammock. You can meet him anywhere. Be creative. Maybe you will find lots of favorite spots to talk with God.

Dear God, you are everywhere, and that's amazing!
Thank you for wanting to be with me.

MARCH 18

Waiting Patiently

If we look forward to something we don't yet have, we must wait patiently and confidently.

ROMANS 8:25 NLT

Some road trips can feel like you are stuck in the car *forever*! Usually you are heading somewhere fun, like to visit friends or family or to discover something new.

You will spend a lot of your life doing cool things, but you will also spend a lot of time waiting. Waiting in lines to go on rides. Waiting to find out if you made the team or passed a test. Waiting for an answer to your prayers. While you wait, remember that the wait will be worth it.

Dear God, instead of complaining, help me make the best of the times when I must wait.

Real or Fake

"These people show honor to me with words, but their hearts are far from me."

Mark 7:6 NCV

Jesus doesn't like us to pretend to be something we are not. He warned the Pharisees in the Bible more than once about their pride. They acted differently in front of different people.

Real people mean what they say, admit their faults, and practice what they preach. Would you say you are real or fake around others? What would others say about you?

Dear God, you see who I am and know what I'm thinking. Help me to be humble and real.

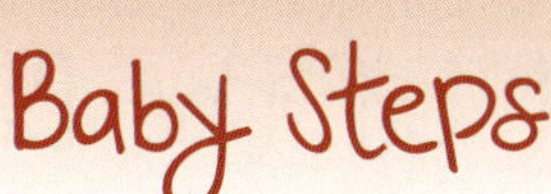

Baby Steps

The LORD makes firm the steps
of the one who delights in him.

PSALM 37:23 NIV

Baby sea turtles are small enough to fit into the palm of your hand, so you can imagine how tiny their little flippers are. Once they dig themselves out of their sand nest, they take tiny steps and inch their way across the sand to the ocean. One step at a time.

Your journey through life can feel like a lot of small steps. Baby steps can lead to something big and exciting. God has good things in store for you.

Dear God, remind me that the choices I make each day are small steps in the right direction.

Part of the Band

How good and pleasant it is
when God's people live together in unity!

PSALM 133:1 NIV

Each person who belongs to the family of God has a part to play in building the kingdom of God. Compare the family of God to a band. When all of the instruments play together, it sounds amazing.

Even though you are young, you still have a part to play. You can be a positive influence in the classroom. You can work well with others on a project. You can pray in a small group.

Dear God, thanks for making me a part of your family. Show me how to work together with others.

Barrel Racing

I will hurry, without delay,
to obey your commands.

PSALM 119:60 NLT

Have you ever seen barrel racing at a rodeo or fair? Horses fly into the arena, heading toward barrels set up in the middle. The riders click their tongue, squeeze their legs and use the reins to guide the horse tightly around each barrel. The rider's instruction works together with the horse's quick response to get through all of the challenges in record time.

Following God's instructions without delay is important to get through challenging situations and finish well. Train yourself to listen to God's prompts and respond right away.

Dear Lord, teach me to be quick to listen and obey.

Beauty and the Pig

A beautiful woman who lacks discretion
is like a gold ring in a pig's snout.

PROVERBS 11:22 NLT

If you think of someone with fine manners and polite eating habits, do you think of a pig? No, never. Pigs aren't the kind of animal you'd walk to an ice cream shop or show off to guests at home. A dog, sure. A cat, maybe. But a pig? Definitely not. Pigs use their snout to root around in dirt for food and roll in mud to protect their skin. You would never see a gold ring in a pig's snout.

Beauty and bad behavior don't go together either. A girl who makes good choices adds to her beauty. Godly beauty shows in how you act.

Dear God, help me to be careful with what I do and say.

Excited to Share

I am not ashamed of the gospel, because it is the power of God that brings salvation to everyone who believes.

Romans 1:16 NIV

When you tell someone about God, you're sharing about the joy you found in Jesus. You aren't forcing anyone to believe what you believe. We are free to do what we want, but there are bad consequences to living like the world does.

The gospel is the good news that Jesus Christ died on the cross to offer forgiveness and salvation to everyone. That's why it is called good news! Jesus loves everyone, and it is their choice to love him back. Be bold and share that good news.

Dear God, I don't want to be ashamed of the gospel. Teach me how to share it with others.

MARCH 25

A Strong Woman

"If you come back to me and trust me, you will be saved. If you will be calm and trust me, you will be strong."

ISAIAH 30:15 ICB

When describing a strong woman, you could say she is a woman who get things done. She is smart and good at figuring out solutions. She doesn't ask other people to do things for her but does it on her own. People admire her.

The Bible describes strength differently. Being patient and waiting for God to lead you instead of pushing ahead without him is actually strong.

Dear Lord, help me to be calm on the inside and trust you. That is true strength.

Hungry

You satisfy me more than the richest feast.
I will praise you with songs of joy.

PSALM 63:5 NLT

There's nothing like a chocolate malt, crispy fries, and a juicy burger. Or maybe you love a big cheesy pizza, or a pile of pasta. Are you hungry for any of those right now?

God filled each of us with desires—the desire for good friends, for fun, for love. He can fill those desires in a way that is deep and lasts forever. It comes from spending time with Jesus.

Dear God, time spent with you is like food to my hungry soul.

The Big Stuff

"God even knows how many hairs are on your head. So don't be afraid."

MATTHEW 10:30-31 NCV

There are many ways to style your hair: cut it, curl it, straighten it, color it. Girls can spend a lot of time and money on their hair. But how big of a deal is hair?

God knows the number of hairs on your head, which is a little thing, and he also knows about the big things, so you don't have to worry. When you brush your hair in the morning, remember that God sees everything and pays close attention to the little stuff and the big stuff. He is in control of it all.

Dear God, if you know all the hairs on my head then I know you care about the details in my life.

The Blame Game

Humble yourselves under the mighty power of God, and at the right time he will lift you up in honor.

1 Peter 5:6 NLT

God made a beautiful garden for Adam and Eve to live in and told them that they could eat fruit from all the trees except for one. They didn't obey, and when God asked them about it, they played the blame game.

Don't make excuses when you disobey. Be humble and admit your part of the problem. Even though it's not easy, it is the first step toward being lifted up to a place of honor where people can trust you to be honest and do what's right next time.

Dear God, help me be humble and deal with my sin without blaming others.

MARCH 29

Blessed

"Now then, my children, listen to me;
blessed are those who keep my ways."

PROVERBS 8:32 NIV

Bless is a word people say often. But what does it mean? A blessing is something good. It's like a gift. God blesses people by giving them good things.

God gives you good things like a nice home, a loving family, good health, and fun stuff, but he also promises comfort for those who are sad and rewards in heaven for staying faithful. Be encouraged to keep doing what is right in God's eyes and receive his blessings.

Dear God, you give me so many things!
You are so good. Thank you.

Easter Resurrection

The angel said to the women. "Don't be afraid. I know that you are looking for Jesus, who has been crucified. He is not here. He has risen from the dead as he said he would."

MATTHEW 28:5-6 NCV

Jesus is the reason we celebrate Easter, but when you walk through stores, you'd think Easter was mostly about jellybeans, chocolate bunnies, candy eggs, and pretty dresses. It's not wrong to have these things at Easter, but you don't want to lose focus on what is most important – Jesus!

What happened at Easter changes everything! You can pray to Jesus because he is alive. You have salvation and forgiveness from sin. You worship a powerful God who defeated death. And you have the hope of eternity in heaven with Jesus. That's the real story of Easter.

Dear God, thank you for all that Easter really means.

Weak Made Strong

"My grace is enough for you. When you are weak, my power is made perfect in you."

2 CORINTHIANS 12:9 NCV

Can you think of someone who is weak? Maybe they don't win very often when you are playing games. They might be quiet or shy. They might not know the answers to the teacher's questions. Although they look weak on the outside, God can give them his power and make them strong on the inside.

When you are weak in an area it can be a chance for God to show you his power. Don't feel bad if you aren't able to do something. Ask God to shine through you.

Dear God, help me know when to ask for your strength.

APRIL

"The joy of the LORD makes you strong."

NEHEMIAH 8:10 NIRV

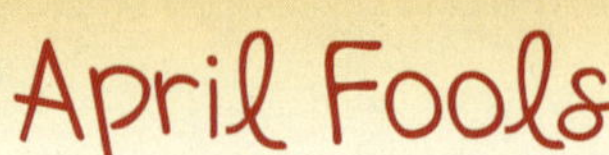

APRIL 1

April Fools

The Lord has glory and majesty.
He has power and joy in his Temple.

1 CHRONICLES 16:27 ICB

It's April Fool's Day, a day when some people play jokes and try to fool each other. Do you think God has a sense of humor? The Bible says there is joy in his presence.

Look at what God created. He made elephants with a six-foot nose and big ears, and giraffes with necks as long as their legs. He made you with tickle spots and funny bones. God is fun.

Dear God, thank you for joy and laughter. I can't wait to see you laugh someday in heaven.

It Won't Last Long

Don't wear yourself out trying to get rich;
be wise enough to control yourself.
Wealth can vanish in the wink of an eye.

PROVERBS 23:4-5 NCV

Money is like candy. It's fun for a little while, but it doesn't last long. Toys break, you outgrow those shoes, and markers dry out. It's fun while it lasts, but things don't last. And then you want something new or better.

Jesus said instead of trying to get rich on earth, where stuff can break, store up treasure in heaven where it will last. Put your energy and time into friendships, family, happy memories, and helping others. Those are the things that last.

Dear God, show me how to control myself and enjoy things that have meaning.

APRIL 3

Be Bold

Sinners run away even when no one is chasing them.
But those who do what is right are as bold as lions.

PROVERBS 28:1 NIRV

Have you ever been so afraid your heart started racing, your hands got sweaty, and your legs felt too heavy to move? When your faith in God leads you to do something bold or daring, stand up and speak up! It can be tough, but when you are bold, things begin to change.

God sees you doing tough things for him, and that makes his heart happy.

Dear Lord, teach me to be confident
in doing what's good and right.

What Really Matters

Has not the one God made you? You belong to him in body and spirit.

MALACHI 2:15 NIV

Do you worry about how you look and what other people will think of you? Do you act a certain way to get noticed? No one else's opinion of you should be so important that you change who you are.

You are God's creation; you belong to him. His opinion of you matters the most. Ask God what he wants for your life. When you put God first, things will fall into place.

Dear God, I want to consider what you think of me over what other people think.

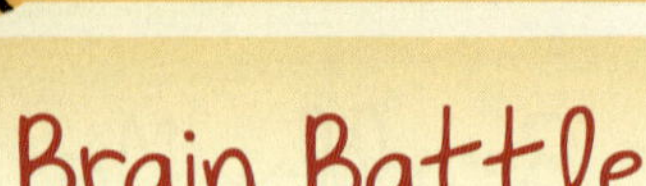

Brain Battle

You will keep in perfect peace
all who trust in you,
all whose thoughts are fixed on you!
ISAIAH 26:3 NLT

Sometimes you just need a break. Your days get filled with homework, chores, lessons, or activities, and you'd rather flop down on your bed in front of a screen.

When you focus your thoughts on God, the result is peace. When you focus on everything you have to get done, the result is worry and fear. Fill your mind with God's promises and fight the bad thoughts and feelings that come up.

Dear God, help me stop my restless thoughts
and rest in your peace.

APRIL 6

Relationship Test

An honest answer
is like a kiss of friendship.
PROVERBS 24:26 NLT

Being honest and truthful makes relationships stand strong. Dishonesty wears away at them. When someone doesn't tell the truth—even once—how can you trust that they won't do it again?

If someone always tells the truth, you can count on them to keep a secret, follow through with a promise, and be honest. Be sure that you are the kind of person other people can trust.

Dear God, help me choose friends who are honest.

APRIL 7

Building Up

Encourage one another and build each other up.

1 THESSALONIANS 5:11 NIV

It feels good when someone gives you a compliment or tells you what a great job you are doing. When you get stuck or frustrated with a task it is helpful to have someone come alongside you and encourage you to keep going and not give up.

You need people in your life who will remind you of what you can do. Be an encourager and look for times to build others up when they feel down.

Dear God, show me ways that I can build my friends up when they're feeling discouraged or down.

Not Fair

Wait and trust the LORD.
Don't be upset when others get rich
or when someone else's plans succeed.

PSALM 37:7 NCV

Sometimes bad people break the law and get rich. Sometimes good people try really hard, follow all the rules, and are still poor. Life is not always fair, and it can be very upsetting. But it's not worth getting mad or letting yourself feel jealous.

The best reaction to stop yourself from getting upset is to pray and then trust God with the rest. He sees what's going on. He will reward you either here on earth or in heaven. You won't miss out.

Dear God, help me turn my bad feelings over to you and trust you to handle things that aren't fair.

No Complaining

Do everything without complaining or arguing.

PHILIPPIANS 2:14 ICB

God had to listen to the people of Israel complaining for forty years in the desert. They complained about living in the desert, about the water, about the food, about a lot of things. Over and over God provided for their needs, but that didn't stop them from complaining.

Complaining shows that you don't trust someone and that you are not grateful. All those negative words don't fix the problem. Let people know what you appreciate and work together to make things better.

Dear God, help me not to create a bad habit of complaining. I want to show people that I am thankful.

APRIL 10

Picture Perfect

Everyone has sinned; we all fall short of God's glorious standard. Yet God, in his grace, freely makes us right in his sight. He did this through Christ Jesus.

ROMANS 3:23-24 NLT

Perfect pictures have been fixed digitally to cover up and change parts that aren't perfect. But no one is perfect even if they look like they are. Only God is perfect. He has never done anything wrong.

Humans aren't capable of being perfect. If you do something wrong, whether on purpose or not, tell God you're sorry and ask for his forgiveness. He doesn't just cover it up. He helps you change.

Dear God, thank you for your grace that will forgive me and wipe away my sin.

APRIL 11

Candyland

It was by faith that Noah built a large boat to save his family from the flood. He obeyed God, who warned him about things that had never happened before.

HEBREWS 11:7 NLT

As much as you'd like to visit a place called Candyland, you know it's not real. If someone said Candyland really existed, you wouldn't believe them. When God told Noah it was going to rain and water would cover the earth, that would have sounded unbelievable. It had never rained before.

What if Noah hadn't believed God and ignored what he said? God was so pleased with Noah's obedience that he saved Noah and his whole family. You won't always understand what God says, but he can always be trusted.

Dear God, help me believe even though I may not understand what you are saying or doing.

Go

"Go everywhere in the world, and tell the Good News to everyone."

MARK 16:15 NCV

God sent Jonah to Nineveh where the people were bad. Jonah wasn't happy about it, but he finally went—after hiding on a boat, being stuck in a terrible storm, getting swallowed by a whale, and then being spit out three days later. But something wonderful happened. The people of Nineveh listened to Jonah and decided to follow God.

There may be mean kids you don't want to talk to. But God loves them, so ask him to give you the words to say and to change your heart toward them.

Dear God, I want to share the good news about your love with those who need it most.

APRIL 13

A Moment or Forever

Truth will last forever.
But lies last only a moment.
PROVERBS 12:19 ICB

An embarrassing moment can happen in just a second, but you remember it forever. Lies can be like that. Have you even been caught telling a story that wasn't true? People will stop trusting what you say if you lie.

A quick lie can run out of control, and it can take forever to earn someone's trust back. So be careful not to lie in the moment and save yourself a lot of trouble in the future.

Dear God, when I'm tempted to lie,
help me remember that it is not worth it.

APRIL 14

Go With Me

She is clothed with strength and dignity.

PROVERBS 31:25 NLT

Sometimes it's hard to have the courage to do the right thing. There is a woman in the Bible named Deborah. She was a strong leader and wasn't afraid to stand up to those who were doing wrong.

What is your reaction when someone asks for help standing up against what's wrong? You may feel unsure at first. It's ok to take a minute to think about what they are asking you to do. God can give you strength and make you feel brave.

Dear God, I don't want to be too afraid to do the right thing. Fill me with strength and go with me.

Feelings Don't Decide

Wait for the LORD.
Be strong and don't lose hope.
PSALM 27:14 NIRV

Esther was beautiful and rich, and she was the queen. It sounds like a fairy-tale life, but Esther was far from her hometown. She missed her family and friends. Instead of sitting around crying, she made the best of her strange, new surroundings.

Courage isn't how you feel; it's what you do. Don't let your feelings decide what you will do. Do what you need to do knowing God is with you and he will help you.

Dear Lord, remind me to come to you
when I need courage.

APRIL 16

Creatively You

LORD, you have made many things;
with your wisdom you have made them all.
The earth is full of your riches.

PSALM 104:24 NIV

God paints beautiful sunsets in orange, pink, and purple. He spreads colorful rainbows across the sky. There are bright fish in the ocean and birds of all colors. But people are God's favorite creation. He carefully shapes each person.

You are one of God's most special creations. The Bible says you are fearfully and wonderfully made. God can show his creativity through the way you think and imagine. He made you amazing.

Dear God, you made so many things.
The earth is full of your riches, and that includes me!

APRIL 17

Excelling

Since you excel in everything—in faith, in speech, in knowledge, in complete earnestness and in the love we have kindled in you—see that you also excel in this grace of giving.

2 CORINTHIANS 8:7 NIV

It's fun to surprise people by doing nice things for them. Think of something your mom would appreciate you doing like washing the dishes, but don't just wash the dishes in the sink. Wash all the dishes, wipe down the sink, the counter, and the table. If you're going to do something, do it well.

When you do something, you can do just what's asked, or you can excel at it. When you give your best, you can be proud, knowing you've done things with excellence.

Dear God, I want to give you and others my very best.

APRIL 18

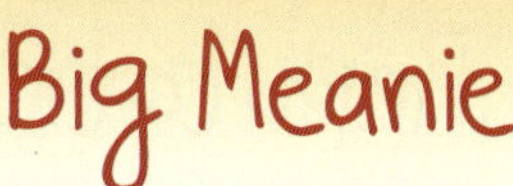

Big Meanie

Hatred stirs up conflict,
but love covers over all wrongs.

PROVERBS 10:12 NIV

You can't always avoid conflict. Grown-ups, kids, Christians or not, everyone has disagreements. A sibling pushes you. A neighbor says something mean. A classmate tells a lie. You may be tempted to hurt them or begin to hate them in your heart.

Take a minute to ask God to help you respond the right way and try to keep things from getting worse. Once you have tried to make things right, forgive them even if you don't feel like they deserve it. Love will help you deal with the wrong.

Dear God, help me guard my heart from hatred and forgive instead.

A Reputation

Choose a good reputation over great riches;
being help in high esteem is better than silver or gold.

PROVERBS 22:1 NLT

You've probably been told many times not to worry about what people think. That's mostly true, but not always. What people think of you does count, and your reputation matters. How you act, what you say, and how you treat others all add to a good or bad reputation.

Write down a few of the things you're known for and put a star by things that are good. Work on doing more good things, so people think highly of you.

Dear God, help me behave in a way
that creates a good reputation.

APRIL 20

Good Gift Giver

Their trust should be in God, who richly gives us all we need for our enjoyment.

1 TIMOTHY 6:17 NLT

What is a gift that you have received that you really enjoyed? Was it something you had been wanting for a while? Was it a total surprise? Have you surprised someone with a gift they really loved?

God loves to give you gifts. Watching you enjoy it puts a smile on his face. Don't be afraid to ask him for things you need or even what you want. He's not bothered by your asking. He is a good father.

Dear God, you fill my life with so many good things. Teach me to give with joy.

APRIL 21

DIY Project

I want to do the things that are good, but I do not do them.

Romans 7:18 NCV

DIY cards, bracelets, and crafts are fun to do, and they save a lot of money. Plus, they let you be creative and make something unique. But when it comes to life projects, you can't just do it yourself. You need God's directions.

Sometimes there's a tug-of-war going on inside you, and you need Jesus' help to change. He loves to help you become better at choosing the right thing. You don't need to do it yourself. Do each day with him.

Dear Jesus, I need your help to change what needs to change in my life.

Don't Worry

Don't worry about anything; instead, pray about everything. Tell God what you need, and thank him for all he has done.

PHILIPPIANS 4:6 NLT

Problems are like magnets. They attract your attention. You think about them, talk about them, worry about them. God says not to worry and to tell him what you need. That's good advice. He knows you need his help. He's ready and waiting.

Write this verse down and hang it somewhere in your room to help you remember to pray and tell God about everything instead of worrying.

Lord, help me to focus on you instead of on my problems. Remind me of all that you've done for me.

He Understands

The Word became human and made his home among us. He was full of unfailing love and faithfulness.

JOHN 1:14 NLT

What if parents had to go to school and stay the whole day, going from class to class, eating in the lunchroom, and playing dodgeball in the gym? Then they would truly understand how you feel at school.

Jesus came down from heaven and lived on earth, so he does understand. He became a human and went through the stuff you go through. When you pray, you're praying to someone who understands.

Dear God, you understand what it's like to live in my world. Thank you for always being with me.

APRIL 24

Spring Cleaning

Let us examine our ways and test them,
and let us return to the LORD.

LAMENTATIONS 3:40 NIV

Clothes on the bed and toys all over the floor. Craft supplies scattered across the desk. Stuffed animals and shoes spilling out of the closet. It's definitely time for spring-cleaning. Every once in a while, you need to go through your room. Pull everything out. Sort it into piles: keep, donate, throw away.

It's good to clean out your life too. Think about what you're busy doing, how well you are doing it, and what needs to change? Sort it out. Make a list. Set goals for anything you need to change.

Dear God, help me examine what I'm doing and show me what needs to change.

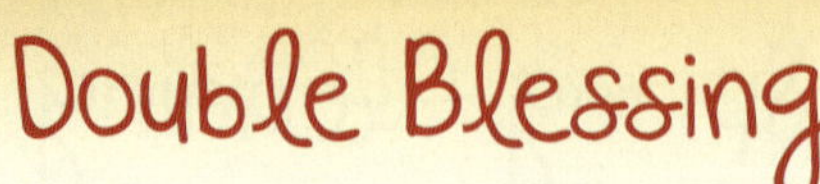

Double Blessing

Because we loved you so much, we were delighted to share with you not only the gospel of God but our lives as well.

1 THESSALONIANS 2:8 NIV

A missionary family invited a village girl they knew to move to the city with them, so she could go to school. Each day the family read the Bible and learned about God. One day the girl realized God was real and that he loved her very much, so she decided to follow Jesus.

Because of the Christian family, the village girl got a great education, and she got to know Jesus. She got a double blessing. You don't have to travel all across the world to share about Jesus. You can bless people with the love of God by sharing what you have.

Dear God, help me to know how to share your good news right where I am.

Great Advice

Plans go wrong for lack of advice;
many advisers bring success.
PROVERBS 15:22 NLT

Parties are fun, but they can be a lot of work. It is helpful to plan ahead with people who have done it before and can give you good advice. It is also helpful to have other people help.

The same thing is true when it comes to making decisions. Instead of feeling like you need to know it all, ask for the experience others have to offer. Parents, teachers, and coaches have more life experience. They might have a different perspective and can help you think through something you hadn't thought of before. If you want plans that succeed, get some advice.

Dear God, remind me to ask for advice when I am planning things.

More Friends

We know that in all things God works for the good of those who love him. He appointed them to be saved in keeping with his purpose.

ROMANS 8:28 NIRV

Have you ever had to move somewhere new? It might sound exciting to begin with, but then you realize you will miss your friends. You might hate it at first. It can be scary not knowing anyone until you make new friends. Friendship is a gift. A friend can make you feel really happy.

As a friend, you can make a difference in someone else's life. Look for someone new. Reach out any way you can to include them. You can help them feel accepted and find more friendships.

Dear God, help me to notice who needs to make new friends and make me bold to go talk to them.

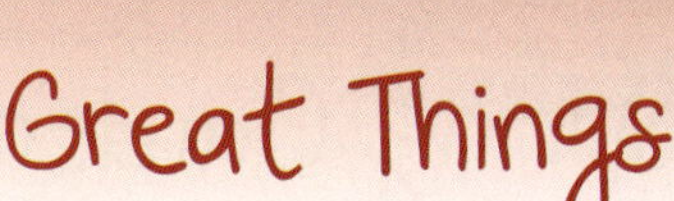

Great Things

"Anyone who believes in me will do the same works I have done, and even greater works."

JOHN 14:12 NLT

What can you do when you hear someone is sick, hurt, or needs help? Ask God for some ideas. Maybe you could have your parents help you make a meal. You could put together a basket of goodies, mow someone's lawn, walk their dog, water their plants, or take out their trash.

God's plan all along was for you to do great things. You don't have to do it all on your own though. Join with others. God can use you in big and small ways to do great things for others.

Dear God, you are so great! Show me the great things you want me to be a part of.

Spring Garden

Humbly accept the word planted in you, which can save you.

James 1:21 NIV

Some families plant a garden in the spring. They dig up the dirt, make rows, and drop in seeds that will someday produce fruits and vegetables. What would you grow in your garden? If the dirt or soil isn't good, then the plants won't grow.

Listening and accepting what God says is like having good soil for seeds of God's Word that grow into something beautiful.

Dear God, I want to be a garden with good soil, so the seeds of your Word will grow and produce fruit in me.

Robin's Nest

You might sleep a little or take a little nap.
You might even fold your hands and rest.

PROVERBS 24:33 NIRV

Have you seen a bird building a nest? For days, a robin will carry small twigs or pieces of grass in her beak. Bit by bit, a nest starts to take shape. The little bits the robin brings add up to a whole lot.

A little sleep, a little rest can turn into late homework, a messy room, and a lot of wasted time. Be on your guard and remember that a little rest is ok, but bit by bit you can get your work done.

Dear God, help me to keep at it and not get lazy when it comes to getting my work done.

MAY
“I will make you strong
and will help you.
I will support you
with my right hand
that saves you.”
Isaiah 41:10 ICB

Do Your Part

Each part does its own work to make the whole body grow and be strong with love.

EPHESIANS 4:16 NCV

God is so smart. He has made so many people, and he has a plan for each one. He made you good at some things and not so good at others. Figure out what you are good at. Make a list. Some things you might get better at with time.

We are all part of the body of Christ. Each part has its own work to do, and all the parts work together. Every part is important to make the whole body work well.

Dear God, show me how you made me to be a part of the body of Christ.

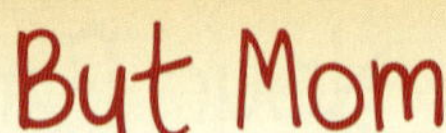

But Mom

Honor your father and your mother. The Lord your God has commanded you to do this. Then you will live a long time. And things will go well for you in the land.

DEUTERONOMY 5:16 ICB

Before you do something, do you want to understand why? That's normal, but sometimes you won't understand. In those times, you need to trust that your parents have a good reason. You may not get it now, but you might when you're older.

Honor your parents and obey them whether you understand it or not. It's more important to God that you obey than understand why.

Dear God, even when I don't understand why, help me to obey my parents.

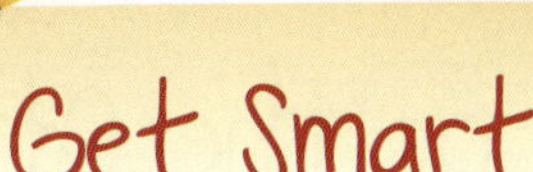

MAY 3

Get Smart

I have more insight than my teachers,
for I am always thinking of your laws.

PSALM 119:99 NLT

This verse isn't saying you know more than your teachers or your coach. This verse is talking about wisdom that comes from God. He can help you understand difficult people and tricky situations. If you're filling your brain with God's truth, he will show you things that other people might miss.

When you learn about God through his Word, you'll be able to understand things in a way that you never could on your own. So, get smart and plug in to his Word.

Dear God, remind me to study your Word to learn your truth and get your thoughts.

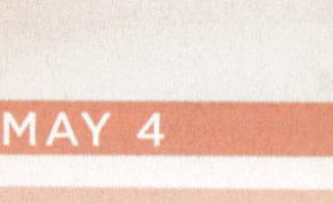

One or the Other

We use our tongues to praise our Lord and Father, but then we curse people, whom God made like himself.

JAMES 3:9-10 NCV

You can't pick pears from an apple tree or blueberries from a strawberry plant. It just doesn't make sense. What would your mom say if you wore your new white shoes to church and then ran around in the playground in the same new white shoes?

But that's what sometimes happens with our mouths. We sing songs to God at church and then say bad words the next day. Is it okay to play with a friend at school and then say mean things about her at your other friend's house? Be careful with what you say and use your tongue only for good.

Dear Lord, help me guard my heart and what comes out of my mouth.

Celebrate

The LORD has done it on this day.
Let us be joyful today and be glad.
PSALM 118:24 NIRV

Some days are worth celebrating. Maybe it is a special day where something important happened, like a birthday or wedding. God likes to celebrate, and he wants you to have fun.

The next time a celebration comes up, join in. Help decorate, clean the house, set up a party room, and thank God for his goodness that is part of your celebration.

Dear God, thank you for giving me
a lot of reasons to celebrate.

MAY 6

Listen to your father, who gave you life,
and do not forget your mother when she is old.

PROVERBS 23:22 NCV

When your parents were kids, things looked different, but they probably had some of the same things happen to them that have happened to you. Ask them if they ever argued with siblings or friends. Did they ever get in trouble with their parents? What were they afraid of?

Take some time to talk to your parents about what their childhood was like. Ask questions about their experiences. They have a lot of wisdom to pass along, and it's good to listen to that.

Dear God, thank you for my family.
Protect them and keep them healthy.

MAY 7

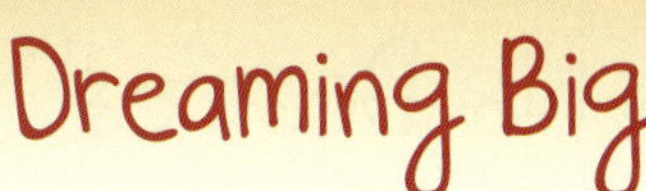

God is able to do far more than we could ever ask for or imagine. He does everything by his power that is working in us.

EPHESIANS 3:20 NIRV

If you could fill a day with your favorite things, people, and places, what would it look like? No matter how big you dream, God can do more. Trying to describe or measure what God is able to do will blow your mind. Your brain can't handle it.

God made an amazing plan so everyone who believes in Jesus can be part of his big family. You are a part of God's dream to help bring everyone into relationship with him.

Dear God, my dreams aren't even close to what you can do. Show me the big things you can do.

MAY 8

His Desires

"Lord, please hear my prayer! Listen to the prayers of those of us who delight in honoring you. Please grant me success today by making the king favorable to me. Put it into his heart to be kind to me."

NEHEMIAH 1:11 NLT

Sometimes God puts a desire inside you to help someone or do something, and you can't stop thinking about it. It's his desire for you to do his important work in the world.

Has God put something on your heart like that? Pay attention to when your heart gets stirred up about something. It might not be right now or even for a few years but watch to see how God will use you to make a difference.

Dear God, please use me to do your work in the world.

Dumb Stuff

Anger will not help you live the right kind of life God wants. So put out of your life every evil thing and every kind of wrong.

JAMES 1:20 NCV

When you're angry, you can say and do dumb things. Acting out when you're angry is the wrong way to respond. Nothing good comes from letting your bad feelings come out the wrong way. The Bible even warns about it.

When you feel anger bubbling up inside, you need to show self-control and keep a lid on it. Train yourself to ask God for help. His Spirit living in you can help you control your anger.

Dear God, please teach me the right way to respond when I am angry.

Everybody Is Doing It

Did I keep my heart pure for nothing?
Did I keep myself innocent for no reason?

PSALM 73:13 NLT

Everybody is doing it. They're lying to their parents, swearing, watching movies you're not allowed to watch, and texting late at night. Do you wonder why you should bother doing what's right when other people are having fun and getting away with it?

Knowing the whole picture will help you avoid giving in to wrong thinking. God is good, fair, and just. He will gently lead you away from wickedness and take care of you. Hang in there and stay strong. It'll pay off in the end to keep your heart pure.

Dear Lord, help me remember the reward you have for those who do what is right.

MAY 11

Eyes Wide Open

Praise the Lord, everything he has created
everything in all his kingdom.
Let all that I am praise the Lord.

Psalm 103:22 NLT

Take a walk around your neighborhood one day and notice the shape of the clouds, the squirrels bouncing around the tree branches, birds flying overhead, ducks swimming in the pond, grasshoppers on the sidewalk, and maybe a butterfly fluttering along. Sometimes it's the little things that make you smile.

You can miss them if you're in a hurry or if you spend too much time with your face in your phone. Ask God to open your eyes to his wonder and then look around at all the living, moving things he shows you.

God, open my eyes to the little things that are amazing.
Thank you for each one.

Face Forward

The righteous keep moving forward,
and those with clean hands become stronger and stronger.

JOB 17:9 NLT

Imagine going through a day without facing forward. Walking to the bus stop. Stepping onto the bus. Practicing piano. Pushing a friend on the swing set. That would feel crazy, and you might get hurt. You were made to face forward. That's one reason why your nose, ears, mouth, and eyes are not on the back of your head.

In life, you can't go back. You can only move forward. You can't control what's behind. But the world has lots of possibilities. Keep moving forward.

Dear God, help me face forward toward the great possibilities you have ahead.

Faith in Action

A brother or sister in Christ might need clothes or might need food. And you say to him, "God be with you! I hope you stay warm and get plenty to eat." You say this, but you do not give that person the things he needs. Unless you help him, your words are worth nothing.

JAMES 2:15-16 ICB

Some people see a need and talk about it. Others do something about it. If you believe in God, then show it. Anyone can talk about what's wrong in the world, but only some step up and use God's power to do something.

People will know what you believe by the good deeds you do. Faith requires action.

Dear God, I want my faith to show, so people will know that I believe in you.

Important Time

Daniel… went home to his upstairs room where the windows opened toward Jerusalem. Three times a day he got down on his knees and prayed, giving thanks to his God, just as he had done before.

DANIEL 6:10 NIV

Each day is busy with all the things you need to do, but there's nothing more important—and amazing—than getting to spend time with your Heavenly Father.

You can spend time with God by thanking him for helping you. Confess what you've done wrong. Read your Bible. Tell God what you need. Pray for others. Quiet your mind and listen to him speak to your heart.

Dear Lord, thank you for taking time to meet with me.

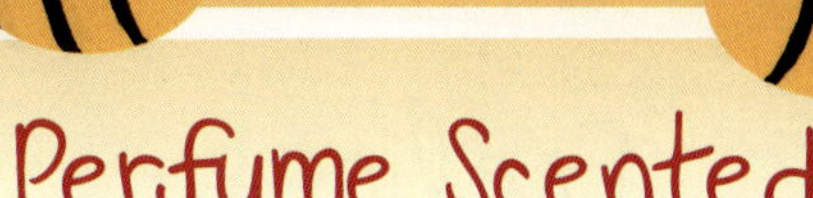

MAY 15

Perfume Scented

The LORD is far from the wicked,
but he hears the prayers of the righteous.

PROVERBS 15:29 NLT

Do you ever stop at the perfume counter and smell the perfume? Some smell lovely and others will make you wrinkle your nose and turn away. God has smells he likes too, not in perfumes but in prayers.

When someone who does right prays, God leans in to listen. When your heart is pure, he hears and answers. Bad attitudes smell bad to God. Next time you smell perfume, whisper a pleasing prayer to God.

Dear God, thank you for listening to me when I pray.

MAY 16

Feelings

When I am afraid,
I put my trust in you.
Psalm 56:3 NIV

The psalms are packed with emotions like sadness, fear, and frustration. God created everyone with emotions. It's what you do with your feelings that can help you or get you stuck.

Don't feel ashamed of your feelings or try to ignore them. You can trust God. He sent the Holy Spirit to comfort you. His Word has good advice on what to do and what not to do. You don't have to hide your feelings from God. You can be honest and tell him all about it.

Dear God, when I feel sad or mad or afraid, remind me to put my trust in you by sharing how I feel.

Praise Dance

Let them praise his name with dancing
and make music to him with timbrel and harp.

PSALM 149:3 NIV

God's chosen people, the Israelites loved to dance while they praised the Lord. What instruments are at your church? Do you play any instruments?

Let the joy inside of you burst out when you worship God. Celebrate all the good things he has done for you. Don't be shy. Your praise dance looks beautiful to God, and he is the one you want to please.

Dear God, help me to praise you with all of me.

MAY 18

You Are Free

We have freedom now, because Christ made us free.
So stand strong.

GALATIANS 5:1 NCV

The older you get, the more freedom you get. Your parents might let you stay up later at night. Your teacher might trust you with a special task. And if you don't make wise choices, you can risk losing those freedoms.

Freedom isn't something you get so you can do whatever you want. The freedom Jesus gives is freedom from sin so you can do what's good. It gives you power, so use it to do good things for God.

Dear Jesus, thank you for giving me freedom.
Show me how to use it to serve you.

MAY 19

He Is Rich

My God will meet all your needs according to the riches of his glory in Christ Jesus.

PHILIPPIANS 4:19 NIV

God is good at taking care of your needs. He is like a rich king with a big heart, but he waits for you to ask him. And don't worry about asking too often. There's no end to what God can give you when your heart is right. He is happy to give you what you need.

God wants to hear from you each day. You can add items to your list and cross off the ones God provides. Watch how God will meet your needs from his riches.

Dear God, the whole earth is yours and everything in it. Help me see your blessing my life.

Free to Be Me

God created human beings in his own image.
In the image of God he created them;
male and female he created them.

GENESIS 1:27 NLT

What do you want to be when you grow up? A teacher? A veterinarian? A mom? A doctor? You have so many choices. God created you to be like him, and that will look different to each person.

Think about how God made you. You have likes and dislikes that will affect which activities you join, what books you read, what college you go to, and what job you will have. Be free to be who God created you to be.

Dear God, you created me in your image,
and I want to be like you.

MAY 21

Good Better Best

Pay careful attention to your own work, for then you will get the satisfaction of a job well done, and you won't need to compare yourself to anyone else.

GALATIANS 6:4 NLT

What is your best? Would that be winning first place in a race? Or getting eight of the ten spelling words correct on a test? Or making a card that your mom really loves? It means trying really hard to do something well.

Comparing yourself to others can make you feel like your best isn't good enough. Don't fall into that trap. Focus on working and you can go from good to better to best.

Dear God, I want to do things really well.
Help me focus on doing my best.

MAY 22

Envy

Love is kind. It does not want what belongs to others.

1 CORINTHIANS 13:4 NIRV

Do you know what the word *envy* means? It's when someone wants something you have, and they are mad at you for having it. Envy can make a person feel miserable.

When you're feeling envious, remind yourself that you don't deserve everything you want or even what someone else has. Thank God out loud for what you do have right now. Being grateful helps chase envy away.

Dear God, thank you for all that I have.
I don't want to have any envy in me.

Great Stone Walls

A person without self-control
is like a city with broken-down walls.
PROVERBS 25:28 NLT

Back in the times of castles and kings, stone walls were built around cities to protect the people inside. They were built high and long to stop enemies from attacking. Enemies would look for weak points to get through. When you don't have self-control, it's like you have weak spots in the wall of protection around your heart and mind.

When you have self-control, you control yourself. You don't let other people or feelings control you. Practice self-control and protect your heart. Don't you feel strong knowing you can do this?

Dear God, thank you for giving me strength
to control myself.

Good Enough

We are made right with God by placing our faith in Jesus.

ROMANS 3:22 NLT

Sometimes it's tempting to rush through a task and not do a good job. You don't give it your best effort. And sometimes you try and try, and it still doesn't turn out well.

If you are trying to be perfect so God will love and accept you, you'll end up feeling like giving up. The great news is you don't have to earn his perfect love. Jesus died on the cross so you can have a relationship with God. Even when you mess up, he still loves you.

Dear God, thank you for loving me and not expecting me to be perfect.

MAY 25

On the Way

My help comes from the Lord,
who made heaven and earth!

Psalm 121:2 NLT

As soon as you call 9-1-1, help is on the way. You can have confidence that the operator will send help. Now think of what happens when you call God by praying. Doesn't he also send help when you pray and ask?

The God who created heaven and earth is ready to help you. That's a lot of help! Ask for help with confidence today.

Dear God, when I call, you answer.
Thank you for watching over me.

MAY 26

Google It

All Scripture is inspired by God and is useful for teaching, for showing people what is wrong in their lives, for correcting faults, and for teaching how to live right.

2 TIMOTHY 3:16 NCV

Do you want to know what the weather will be like tomorrow? Google it. Want to know how long it will take to get to your friend's house? Google it. Search engines can find the information you want with the click of a button.

The whole Bible is inspired by God. It is like a search engine that has answers for life. Struggling with fear? Want to know how to get along with others? Not sure what decision to make? God's Word will lead you to the answer.

Dear God, thank you for showing me in your Word how to live a good life.

Truly or Twisted

Buy the truth and don't sell it.
Get wisdom, instruction and understanding as well.
PROVERBS 23:23 NIRV

Have you ever saved up for something you really wanted? Did it take you a long time to save up? Because you wanted that item so badly, you probably treasured it once you got it.

This verse in Proverbs, the book of wisdom, explains how important truth is. You don't want truth from the world. You want to hear God's truth that hasn't been twisted. Read your Bible so you know the difference between God's truth and the world's lies.

Dear God, building my life on truth is something I don't want to ever let go of.

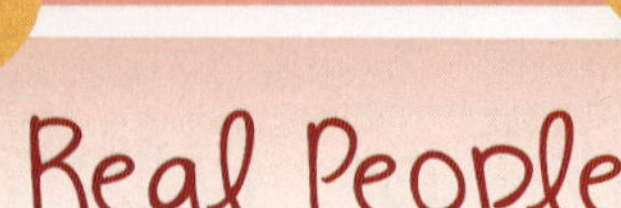

MAY 28

Real People

When God's people are in need, be ready to help them.

ROMANS 12:13 NLT

There was a family at church who went through a really hard time after the dad lost his job. They didn't have enough money to pay their bills or buy groceries or fix their car when it broke. Some ladies at church made meals and dropped off groceries each week. A mechanic at church fixed their car without charging the family. Another lady knew about an open position at her work and helped the dad get a new job.

God uses real people to help others. Pray about what you can do to be part of the solution.

Dear God, open my eyes to see people who need help.

MAY 29

Trash Talk

"When the Spirit of truth comes, he will guide you into all truth. He will not speak on his own but will tell you what he has heard."

JOHN 16:13 NLT

You know that telling the truth is important. But do you tell the truth to yourself or choose to believe lies? When people say unkind things about you, do you believe them?

When you give your life to Jesus, his Holy Spirit lives inside of you. He only speaks truth, so you know that none of the bad thoughts you have about yourself are true. Tell them to leave in Jesus' name and replace them with God's truth.

Dear Lord, help me not to let lies stay in my head and make me feel bad about myself. I need your truth.

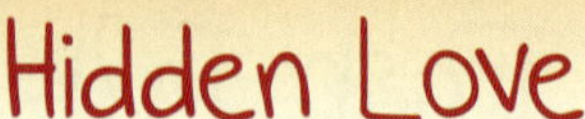

Hidden Love

Better is open rebuke
than hidden love.

PROVERBS 27:5 NIV

Good friends are loyal and kind. You can trust them, and they are fun to be with. They like you the way you are. Friends laugh together, and they can be honest with each other. People don't always want to hear that they are doing something wrong. The Bible calls that *rebuke*.

Loving somebody isn't always about telling them how wonderful they are. Sometimes you have to correct them in love. Find friends who can be open and honest with you.

Dear God, please help my friendships
to be full of honesty and love.

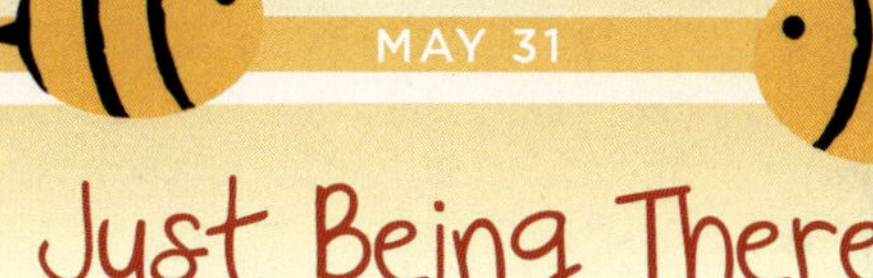

MAY 31

Just Being There

Give praise to the Lord. Give praise to God our Savior.
He carries our heavy loads day after day.

PSALM 68:19 NIRV

Are you the type of girl who likes to talk to your mom about your day? Talk about what happened at school, on the bus, at practice. Talk about your problems or mistakes. Talk about what you're afraid of and what you hope for. It feels good to have someone sit with you and listen to you talk it out.

Sometimes you just need someone who will listen and remind you that things will be okay. God is always with you. Talk to him about how you're feeling. Let him take care of what you are worried about.

Dear God, I know I can talk to you anytime
and you listen. Thank you.

JUNE

"The LORD gives me strength
and protects me.
He has saved me."

EXODUS 15:2 NIRV

Hello Summer

You set the boundaries of the earth,
and you made both summer and winter.

PSALM 74:17 NLT

What a great feeling it is to roll out of bed after you've slept in and know that you can do whatever you want because it's summer! Sun and flipflops. Swimming and sandcastles. Ice cream and watermelon. Picnics and beach days. God put so many good things into summer.

As you start off your summer, think about what you'd like to do over the next few months. You have lots of extra time, so make some fun plans and enjoy this season God made.

Dear God, I love summer! Thank you for the break from school and for fun times with my friends and family.

Hiding Place

You are my hiding place;
you protect me from trouble.
You surround me with songs of victory.

PSALM 32:7 NLT

Far up north in the Arctic, mother seals hide their young pups in small caves under the ice. She tries to hide her pups from polar bears that have a very strong sense of smell. The mother seals must be very careful to protect their young pups.

That's an example of how God protects his children. He is a hiding place: a place where you can go when there's trouble.

Dear God, it makes me feel safe to know that you protect me from trouble.

JUNE 3

Deleted Forever

If we confess our sins to him, he is faithful and just to forgive us our sins and to cleanse us from all wickedness.

1 JOHN 1:9 NLT

Deleting is sometimes a bad thing, like when you accidentally delete a favorite photo, or a homework assignment, or a favorite app. But sometimes deleting is a good thing.

Because Jesus died on the cross, God deletes all your sins. When you admit you did something wrong and ask God to forgive you, he hits that delete button and your sin is gone for good.

Dear Jesus, thank you for deleting my sin when I confess it.

Gift of Grace

"I alone—will blot out your sins for my own sake and will never think of them again."

ISAIAH 43:25 NLT

Because Jesus paid the price for your sin by giving his life to die on the cross, he can give you the gift of grace. He forgives you and gives you another chance.

Jesus will wipe out your sins and never think of them again. Then you can pray and talk directly to God. You get a free pass, and you can go to him as many times as you want to. He gives you grace because he loves you.

Dear Jesus, thank you for setting me free from the punishment I deserve and giving me grace instead.

Just like Jesus

Walk in the way of love, just as Christ loved us and gave himself up for us.

EPHESIANS 5:2 NIV

Talking about doing something is easy, but doing it is the hard part. Jesus did what he said. He didn't just tell you what to do; he shows you how through the examples in the Bible. He said, "love others." Then he shows how by accepting people, helping them feel cared for, and giving his life for them.

Could you do the same for someone else? Share the good news of Jesus and show them his love. You can be like Jesus to those around you every day.

Dear Jesus, thank you for showing me how to follow your footsteps.

Jump for Joy

He jumped to his feet and began to walk. Then he went with them into the temple courts, walking and jumping, and praising God.

ACTS 3:8 NIV

In the Bible, there was a man who couldn't walk. He had been sitting on the side of the road begging people for money since he didn't have a job. When he asked Peter and John for money, Peter looked right at him and told him to walk. God made the man's legs strong. He was so happy he started jumping and praising God.

Has God done something special in your life or in the life of someone you know? Don't be afraid to get excited about it. Get up and praise the Lord just like the lame man did.

Dear God, sometimes I'm so happy I want to jump for joy. Thank you for the amazing things you do.

Keep It Simple

A tongue that calms
is like a tree of life.

PROVERBS 15:4 NIRV

When someone is sad, one of the greatest gifts you can give them is these two words: I'm sorry.

Then give them a hug. Sit with them while they cry. You don't have to know what to say to fix it.

Keep it simple. You don't have to stay with them all day. A quick visit or even a call or message to let them know you are thinking about them and praying for them feels good.

Dear God, I want to support those who are hurting. Remind me to be gentle and careful with my words.

The Size of a Gift

"They gave only what they did not need. This woman is very poor, but she gave all she had to live on."

LUKE 21:4 NCV

Jesus and his disciples were at the temple one day as people dropped off their gifts. Some people were in fancy clothes and dropped a lot of money into the offering box. *Clink, clink, clink, clink.* Everyone could hear the coins fall in the slot. Then a very poor woman walked in and gave two small coins. It wasn't much, but Jesus knew it all she had.

The other people had given from the extra money they had. The poor woman gave all that she had. A gift isn't worth more or less depending on how much it costs. What matters is the heart of the one who gave it.

Dear God, teach me to see the heart behind the gift.

Top Three

What does the LORD require of you?
To act justly and to love mercy
and to walk humbly with your God.

MICAH 6:8 NIV

People might ask what your top three of something are. Your top three favorite places to go on vacation. Your top three ice cream flavors. Your top three movies or books. It's fun to ask your friends and family what their top three favorites are.

God has a top three list too. 1. Act justly by doing what is right and fair. Tell the truth. 2. Love mercy by forgiving people when they mess up. 3. Walk humbly. Treat others better than yourself.

Dear God, teach me to act with your top three in mind.

Same but Different

There are different kinds of gifts, but they are all from the same Spirit.

1 CORINTHIANS 12:4 NCV

When God's Spirit is inside you, he gives you gifts. There are different kinds of gifts like teaching, preaching, and healing. There are even gifts that help you know things. Some people are curious and want to know why. Some are good at speaking in front of crowds of people, and some are shy but are good at thinking through ideas and planning.

All of God's gifts are good and useful. How would you describe yourself? Which gifts from God's Holy Spirit would you like to have? You can ask God to give you those gifts.

Dear God, I'm so glad you made us all different. Help me to be grateful for the way you made me.

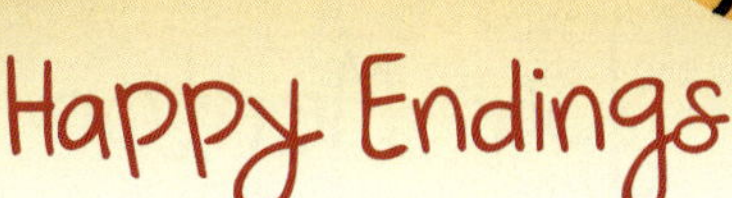

Happy Endings

"God himself will be with them. He will wipe every tear from their eyes, and there will be no more death or sorrow or crying or pain. All these things are gone forever."

REVELATION 21:3-4 NLT

Don't you just love stories that have happy endings? Like a lost animal who finds its way home, or when the bad guys get caught, or people who argue and fight make up and live happily ever after.

It makes you feel better knowing things worked out in the end, but not all stories have happy endings. Sometimes pets get lost. Sometimes the bad guys get away, and some people don't get along. Don't lose hope. God promises a forever happy ending in heaven.

Dear God, thank you for the hope of a happy ending.

JUNE 12

Your Mentor

Remember your leaders who taught you the word of God. Think of all the good that has come from their lives, and follow the example of their faith.

HEBREWS 13:7 NLT

When you need to talk about your feelings, who do you go to? Your mom? A friend? A teacher or a leader at church? God knew you would need other ladies in your life to come alongside you and help you learn about God by being a good example. Those women are called mentors.

You can have mentors who help you learn a skill, who explain things to you, and who help you grow in your faith. God gave you a built-in mentor in your mom, but it's good to have other mentors too. Look for someone you trust and admire. Pray about who God wants to be your mentor.

Dear God, thank you for putting amazing ladies in my life who can be good role models.

He Gets It

The LORD is the Creator of all the earth.
He never grows weak or weary.
No one can measure the depths of his understanding.

ISAIAH 40:28 NLT

God is the Creator of the universe. He is all powerful and all knowing. He completely understands. He never sleeps or misses what is happening in your life.

Instead of looking at your problem, look to God. He sees when you go through hard times and he says, “Look at me. Ask me for help. I’m God. I made this great, big world and everything in it. I can help you.”

Dear God, you understand even when I don’t. Please help me not forget how big and awesome you are.

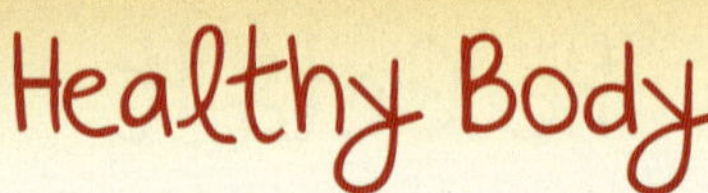

Healthy Body

Don't depend on your own wisdom.
Respect the LORD and refuse to do wrong.
Then your body will be healthy,
and your bones will be strong.

PROVERBS 3:7-8 NCV

Push-ups, sit-ups, jumping jacks, running, all these help your body to be healthy. What you eat makes a difference too. Your parents probably tell you to eat lots of fruit and vegetables because they are full of vitamins and minerals that your body needs. Food, exercise, vitamins, and a good night's sleep all work together in making your body healthy and your bones strong.

Doing what's right and respecting the Lord will make your spirit healthy and strong. God's Word protects you from what's harmful.

Dear Lord, I want to be healthy in my body, mind, and heart. Help me to obey you.

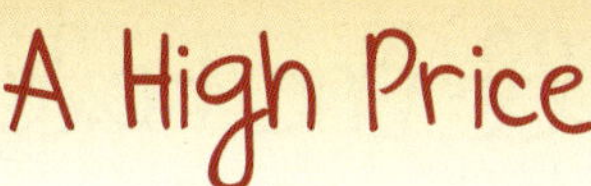

A High Price

You are not your own; you were bought at a price.
Therefore honor God with your bodies.

1 Corinthians 6:19-20 NIV

Jesus left all the riches of heaven and died on the cross to give you eternal life. That's how valuable you are to him. He did it because he loves you. When you ask him into your heart, you become a child of God.

It is amazing to think of how great God's love is for you. How can you honor him for paying such a high price for you?

Dear Jesus, the price you paid on the cross shows me how precious I am to you. Thank you.

Fill the Holes

The believers studied what the apostles taught. They shared their lives together. They ate and prayed together.

ACTS 2:42 NIRV

Some holes need to be fixed or filled, like a hole in your backpack or a hole in the road. It feels good to put in the last puzzle piece. It's fun to insert a key that opens a mysterious door. Donut holes are pretty good too.

God gives you people to share your life with like family, friends, teachers, pastors, and other people who believe in Jesus. All of those people help fill holes in your life. Their love and laughter help fill you up.

Dear God, thank you for my friends, my family, and those at church who fill me up.

JUNE 17

Ice Cream Time

There is a time for everything,
and a season for every activity under the heavens.
He has made everything beautiful in its time.
ECCLESIASTES 3:1, 11 NIV

Summertime is ice cream time. What's your favorite ice cream flavor? Do you like toppings or do you prefer to eat it plain?

There are seasons in life like seasons on earth. Each season has something different about it. There are things you like and things you don't. There are seasons to work, to rest, to play, and to study. Sometimes you are happy and other times you are sad. Try to find what God made beautiful in each season.

Dear God, I believe that your plans are good.

JUNE 18

Trail Ride

"I will guide you along the best pathway for your life.
Do not be like a senseless horse or mule
that needs a bit and bridle to keep it under control."

PSALM 32:8-9 NLT

Going on a horseback ride can be a fun activity. Usually you walk along a path that runs through a forest or maybe beside a river or lake. Most trail horses know the way and clip-clop along slowly. If you tug on the reins, the horse might choose not to obey you.

Sometimes you may have your own ideas about what you want to do. You might not feel like doing what God says. Don't be like the horse who doesn't obey. Let God guide you on the best path for your life.

Dear God, help me trust your way and follow your path for my life.

A Bad Habit

Some of you say, "I have the right to do anything." But not everything is helpful.

1 CORINTHIANS 6:12 NIRV

What would happen if you had two pots of daisies in a sunny spot and you only watered one of them? Without rain or water, flowers will dry up, the petals will fall off, the leaves will turn brown, and the plant will die. If you don't feed something, or water it, it won't grow.

With a habit, the more you do it, the harder it becomes to break, and it will grow stronger. The less you do it, the easier it becomes to break until the habit shrivels up and dies. Pray for God to help you break bad habits.

Dear Lord, I want to remove bad habits from my life. Give me strength to keep at it.

What You Do

Do not worry about anything, but pray and ask God for everything you need, always giving thanks.

PHILIPPIANS 4:6 NCV

Some days don't go well. You forget your lunch at home. Your dog gets off the leash and runs off. Your best friend is sick. Things happen that you don't have control over, and that might make you worry about what will happen next. How do you respond to worry? Breathe.

It's always good to pause and take a deep breath before you react. Take a moment to pray and get God involved. He has the power to help and the wisdom to know what to do.

Dear Lord, when things don't go well, help me pause, breathe, and pray.

I Am

God said to Moses, "I AM WHO I AM. When you go to the people of Israel, tell them, 'I AM sent me to you.'"

EXODUS 3:14 NCV

What do you think God is like? Do you imagine him like a smiley Santa Claus who gives lots of presents? Or a judge who waits for you to do something wrong? How about a strict teacher who taps their foot, crosses their arms, and always frowns? None of those really describe who God is.

Trying to describe God is nearly impossible. He is too perfect, too amazing, too holy. God is everything you need for your whole life.

Dear God, you are perfect, amazing, and holy. Everything I need is found in you.

Can't Wait

LORD, every morning you hear my voice.
Every morning, I tell you what I need,
and I wait for your answer.

PSALM 5:3 NIV

"I can't wait!" Have you said those words while waiting for a fun vacation, or a baby to be born, or to open presents on Christmas? Waiting can be hard, but it can also be exciting. Something good is coming.

You can have the same attitude when you pray. When you ask God for something in prayer, he is listening. While you wait for an answer, don't become impatient and don't lose heart. Expect the best from God!

Dear God, change my heart to expect good things from you and to trust you will answer me.

JUNE 23

Life with Purpose

Since God has shown us great mercy, I beg you to offer your lives as a living sacrifice to him. Your offering must be only for God and pleasing to him.

ROMANS 12:1 NCV

There was a blind man who sat by the side of the road asking for money. He did this all day, so he could get money to buy food. One day Jesus passed by and healed the man. He could see!

Jesus told everyone that the miracle was done to show God's power. The blind man had a purpose, a reason he was blind, so that his healing could show others how amazing God is.

Your life has a purpose, a reason, and meaning too.

Dear God, thank you for giving my life purpose.

JUNE 24

I Wish

He satisfies your desires with good things
so that your youth is renewed like the eagle's.

PSALM 103:5 NIV

What do you secretly wish for? To be funny, to sing well, or to be good at basketball? Do you wish for a really good, best friend, a bedroom of your own, or a brother or sister? God sees the desires of your heart. He knows what you wish for, but he likes it when you tell him yourself.

God doesn't wave a magic wand or grant you three wishes like a genie. He cares about what's in your heart. He likes to talk about your wishes and share good things with you.

Dear God, you know me so well. Thank you for taking time to listen to me share my wishes with you.

JUNE 25

Be like-minded, be sympathetic, love one another, be compassionate and humble.

1 PETER 3:8 NIV

When someone is having a bad day, you have a choice about how you will respond. You can ignore them. Or you can find out what's going on and see how you can help. It's better to show compassion and try to help than to walk away.

One of the best ways to show compassion is to listen. People feel better when they have someone to talk to. You may not understand, and that's okay. They might just need to know someone cares enough to listen.

Dear God, help me be a good listener, especially to someone who is sad or upset.

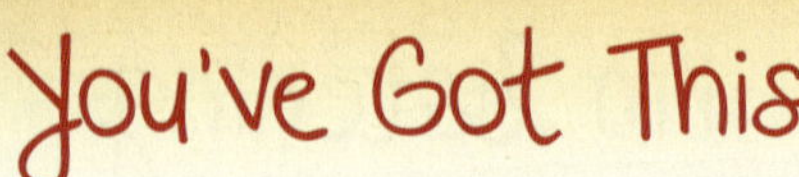

You've Got This

The Spirit God gave us does not make us timid, but gives us power, love and self-discipline. So do not be ashamed of the testimony about our Lord.

2 TIMOTHY 1:7-8 NIV

Some ladies can boldly stand up and speak in front of a group of people. They can make new friends easily. Other people hold back and spend more time thinking about what could go wrong. They may not be sure about what to do or are afraid of making the wrong choice.

God created different personality types—both outgoing and shy. But both types can be confident. That comes from knowing you are a daughter of God. You have his power in you, so you can be bold.

Dear God, give me your power and confidence to share your love no matter how I feel.

Please Help

Our help is in the name of the LORD,
the Maker of heaven and earth.

PSALM 124:8 NIV

People will ask you for help your whole life. Sometimes you play a part in completing a project, and other times you have to do the whole thing yourself.

God is always there to help you. He has all the power to do what needs to be done. You can ask him for what you need and then trust him to take care of it because he's God.

Dear God, thank you are always all the help I need.

Imagination

"God's voice thunders in marvelous ways;
he does great things beyond our understanding."

Job 37:5 NIV

When you go to a movie theatre and the lights go out, you will soon be lost in a world of imagination. Special effects, surround sound, interesting characters, and amazing graphics all come together to tell a story that sucks you in.

God is amazing at using words to help paint a picture in your mind. What word pictures could you use to describe God? Use your imagination and give it a try.

Dear God, thank you for using words to help me picture what you are saying.

Imperfect People

"I live in a high and holy place.
I give new life to those who are humble."

Isaiah 57:15 ICB

There are a lot of imperfect people in the Bible. Cain killed his own brother. Jacob lied to his dad. Moses had an anger problem. Jonah ignored God and ran away. Paul arrested Christians. But God still used each of them to do good.

God uses imperfect people. He loves those who are humble. You don't have to be perfect for God to use you. Have a humble heart that can be honest when you do wrong. God will always forgive you when you're truly sorry.

Dear God, show me how to have a humble heart and ask for forgiveness when I do wrong.

JUNE 30

Not too Young

Don't let anyone look down on you because you are young. Set an example for the believers in what you say and in how you live. Also set and example in how you love and in what you believe.

1 TIMOTHY 4:12 NIRV

Just because you are young, it doesn't mean you can't be a good example for others. You can tell people about God and live in a way that's pleasing to him. Use the power you have to encourage others to do what is right and good.

Don't believe the lie that you are too young to do things for God. You might be just the person he wants to use to change the world.

Dear God, thank you for using me for your kingdom even though I am young.

JULY
The Lord defends those who suffer.
He protects them
in times of trouble.
Psalm 9:9 ICB

Beauty Inside

Fancy hairstyles don't make you beautiful. Wearing gold jewelry or fine clothes doesn't make you beautiful. Instead, your beauty comes from inside you.

1 PETER 3:3-4 NIRV

Sometimes it's fun to dress up in fancy clothes or trendy outfits or even in silly costumes. You can pretend to be someone else. But what matters most is how you look on the inside!

Are you kind to your siblings? Do you only think about yourself? When you look in the mirror think also about your heart. Don't forget to put on love, kindness, and patience today.

Dear God, I want my true beauty to come from my heart not how I look on the outside.

Muddy Water

Letting your sinful nature control your mind leads to death.
But letting the Spirit control your mind leads to life and peace.

ROMANS 8:6 NCV

What's your favorite thing to drink? Lemonade? A strawberry banana smoothie? Hot chocolate? Imagine if you mixed a cup of hot chocolate and a cup of muddy water. How do you think that would taste? Gross. The yummy chocolate would be ruined by the mud.

When you follow God, you can't do what God wants most of the time and what you want some of the time. Don't let even a little bit of sin get mixed into your life because it affects everything.

Dear God, I don't want to let sin in at all.
I need you to help me.

Patient and Gentle

With patience you can convince a ruler,
and a gentle word can get through to the hard-headed.

PROVERBS 25:15 NCV

A woodpecker can peck up to twenty times per second to get at tiny insects buried in the wood. Even though it takes a while, the woodpecker will keep at it. It has patience. You need patience when you're doing schoolwork that's hard, or learning a difficult dance routine, or trying to wash the dog and it keeps shaking.

Patience is also what you need when you're trying to help someone who won't listen. Using gentle words and having patience wins.

Dear God, teach me to be patient in small things and big things.

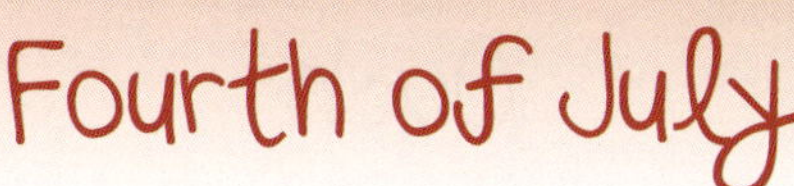

Fourth of July

When I look at the night sky
and see the work of your fingers—
the moon and the stars you set in place—
what are mere mortals that you should think about them,
human beings that you should care for them?

Psalm 8:3-4 NLT

How do you celebrate the Fourth of July? Lake time, pool parties, picnics, barbecues, time with family and friends? The best part is when the night sky lights up with fireworks!

You can see amazing things that God made every day: brilliant sunrises and sunsets, shimmering stars, and changing shapes of the moon. The world is so big, and you are so small, but God still cares more about you than any living thing.

Dear God, thank you for caring about me more than all the other things you have created.

Ouch

Whoever forgives someone's sin makes a friend,
but gossiping about the sin breaks up friendships.

PROVERBS 17:9 NCV

When someone says something mean, it hurts your heart. What you do next can make it worse or help it heal. Telling everyone about it won't help. Thinking about it constantly won't make it better. Choosing to forgive will allow the hurt to heal because forgiveness makes love grow.

Don't let your heart stay hurt. Stop bad thoughts in your mind right away and talk to Jesus. He has the power to make things better.

Dear Lord, help me to let go of hurt
and show forgiveness instead.

Never Give Up

Love never gives up, never loses faith, is always hopeful, and endures through every circumstance.

1 CORINTHIANS 13:7 NLT

Families are made up of a lot of people: grandmas and grandpas, uncles and aunts, cousins, moms and dads, brothers and sisters.

Sometimes the people you love make bad choices. They might need someone to help them, and they will always need family who loves them. That doesn't mean their bad choices are okay. It means you choose to love. Keep praying for them. Never give up believing in the power of God.

Dear God, please show the people in my family your love and remind me not to stop praying for them.

Never Ashamed

Never be ashamed to tell others about our Lord.

2 TIMOTHY 1:8 NLT

When you share great news, you want everyone to be excited with you. When you share the good news about Jesus, some people might listen. Some might not. Some people will accept your invitation to visit your church. Some will make fun of you or ignore you.

Don't stop talking about Jesus. Never be ashamed to tell others about what he has done.

Dear Jesus, give me the courage to keep sharing about you with people who don't know you.

Where You Are

A father is tender and kind to his children.
In the same way, the LORD is tender and kind
to those who have respect for him.

PSALM 103:13 NIRV

God loves you just the way he made you. You aren't exactly like your brother or sister. Your dad isn't exactly like his father. Each person has their own hopes and dreams, abilities and needs.

God is like a good father who tenderly loves and shows kindness to those who respect him. You don't have to be like anyone else.

Dear God, help me to show kindness to others just like you do.

JULY 9

Promises

Your kingdom is an everlasting kingdom,
and your dominion endures through all generations.
The LORD is trustworthy in all he promises
and faithful in all he does.

PSALM 145:13 NIV

When the angel told Sarah she was going to have a baby, she laughed. She was wrinkled and gray and ninety years old. A year later, her baby boy was born. Sarah named him Isaac, which means laughter. God had filled her with joy and kept his promise to her.

God's Word is packed full of his promises. All of the promises you read in the Bible are true. His promises are for you too. You can trust him. He won't break one promise.

Dear God, I can count on you to do what you say.
Thank you.

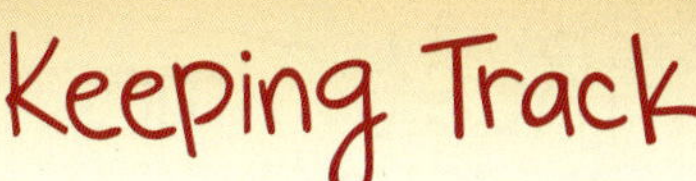

Keeping Track

Love… keeps no record of being wronged.

1 Corinthians 13:4-5 NLT

God doesn't keep track of everything you've done wrong. When you confess your sin, he completely forgives you and calls you free. Remember this when your sister says mean things to you, or your brother plays with your toy without asking, or your friend invites someone else over but not you.

Forgive like God has forgiven you. Don't keep a record of all the bad things. Forgive and move on.

Dear God, when it's hard to forgive, remind me how forgiving you are with me.

Rest Time

"Come to me, all of you who are tired and have heavy loads, and I will give you rest."

MATTHEW 11:28 NCV

There are kids who live in two homes. Because their parents are divorced, they live at their dad's house certain days of the week and then they go live at their mom's house the other days. Sometimes they trade off holidays to spend with their mom one year and their dad the next. That can be tough.

If that's you, Jesus invites you to come to him. You can tell him how you are feeling about anything. He's good at keeping it just between the two of you. You don't have to carry heavy burdens in your heart or in your mind. Let Jesus help you.

Dear Jesus, when I have something tough in my life, show me that you're with me.

Here Comes Trouble

We also have joy with our troubles, because we know that these troubles produce patience. And patience produces character, and character produces hope.

Romans 5:3-4 NCV

Trouble can lead to patience, then character, then hope. Whatever your trouble looks like, God can take your trouble and turn it into good. That doesn't mean what happened isn't hard or sad.

Instead of only focusing on the bad thing, watch God use it for good in your life. You can grow from trouble to having patience to building strong character and hope that you can share with those God puts in your life.

Dear God, the next time trouble comes, I'll use it as a chance to learn to be more like you.

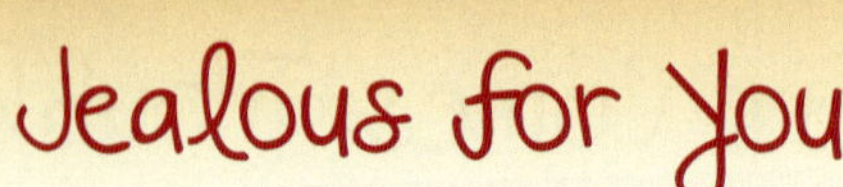

Jealous for You

"The Lord, whose very name is Jealous, is a God who is jealous about his relationship with you."

Exodus 34:14 NLT

There are special people in your life that you have fun hanging out with, but how would you feel if they didn't want to be with you? Probably not very good.

When you give all your time and attention to things that don't include God, how do you think that might make him feel? He loves you so much, and he wants to spend time with you.

Dear God, I want you to be first in my life. Please show me what is taking my attention away from you.

Messy Room

I trust in the LORD.
I will be glad and rejoice in your unfailing love,
for you have seen my troubles.
PSALM 31:6-7 NLT

When people are coming for dinner, you clean up as much as you can. There might be one or two rooms that don't get cleaned. Instead, you just close the door to keep guests from going in there.

Imagine your life is like a house. When Jesus comes into your heart, there's nothing he doesn't see. He knows everything about you. Be honest with him. He will listen. Open the door to your heart and let him come in to help clean up the mess.

Dear God, some things are hard to share.
Remind me that I can talk to you about everything.

JULY 15

Do It for Me

"I tell you the truth. Anything you did for any of my people here, you also did for me."

MATTHEW 25:40 ICB

Do you have a little brother or sister? It's great to have siblings, but sometimes they can be annoying. Because they are younger, they need your help. Moms and dads get busy, and you might need to stop what you're doing to help.

Jesus said that whatever you do to help someone, it's like you are doing it for Jesus. Remember that the next time you're asked to help someone. Do it for Jesus.

Dear Jesus, help me to treat others like I would treat you.

JULY 16

Ripple Effects

The words of thoughtless people cut like swords.
But the tongue of wise people brings healing.

PROVERBS 12:18 NIRV

Skipping rocks from the shore is fun to do. When the rock hits the water, little ripples are created that flow out from the point where the rock hit. The words you say have a ripple effect on those around you. Your words can hurt or heal.

Thoughtless words can hurt. Kind words can bring comfort and hope. Don't forget about the power of your words.

Dear God, help me to speak words that help others instead of hurting them.

JULY 17

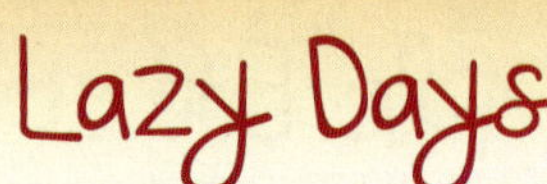

Warn those who are lazy. Encourage those who are timid. Take tender care of those who are weak. Be patient with everyone.

1 THESSALONIANS 5:14 NLT

Part of the fun of summer is lazy days of sleeping in and freedom from a daily schedule. You can sort of do what you want, when you want. It's good to relax and slow down.

It's also good to make sure you don't become lazy. Encourage your friends. Take care of those who are weak. And be patient with everyone. When you have free time, look around you and see who you can help.

Dear Jesus, help me use my time wisely and look for ways I can help people.

What Religion Is

Pure and genuine religion in the sight of God the Father means caring for orphans and widows in their distress and refusing to let the world corrupt you.

JAMES 1:27 NLT

Following God isn't confusing. It's not hard to understand. Take care of people who need help, and don't let the world make you a bad person.

God says religion is loving people and staying away from things you know are wrong. You know in your heart what you should and shouldn't do, so do that. Don't make it harder than it is.

Dear God, thanks for making things simple and showing me what's important.

Bag of Bitterness

Be careful that no one becomes like a bitter weed growing among you. A person like that can ruin all of you.

HEBREWS 12:15 ICB

Some people keep score of all the ways they have been hurt and don't truly forgive. They become grumpy and don't trust people. They carry around a heavy bag of bitterness.

Once you forgive someone, you can let go of the hurt and be free. You might need to talk to them and share your feelings. You might need a grown up to help you talk through it. Do your best to live in peace and try to get along with everyone.

Dear God, help me to forgive even when it hurts a lot. Help me to keep bitterness from growing in my heart.

Know for Yourself

It was your own eyes that saw all these great things the LORD has done.

DEUTERONOMY 11:7 NIV

Have you ever wanted something that your family just couldn't afford? Maybe you even prayed about it and asked the Lord to provide. Then in some special way God made it possible for you to have it.

You can read about the miracles God did in the Bible. People like Moses and Esther and Hannah prayed with all their heart, and God answered their prayers in amazing ways!

Dear God, I know you still answer prayer, and you still do miracles. Let me see you working now.

Laugh a Little

A friend loves at all times.

PROVERBS 17:17 NIV

Everyone has embarrassing moments when things don't go the way you planned. You might feel dumb, stupid, or silly. Don't let those feelings take over.

It is good to be able to laugh at yourself. If someone tries to make fun of you, but you laugh it off instead of getting angry, they might not bother teasing you again. Let joy fill your heart instead of anger and laugh a little.

Dear God, help me to laugh at my silly mistakes instead of being embarrassed or mad.

JULY 22

Run

Run away from the evil desires of youth.

2 TIMOTHY 2:22 NCV

Sometimes you just have to run. Not like running to get to class on time or running to catch the bus or running during soccer practice. Run away when someone is planning to do something wrong, when you're tempted to grab another cookie after your mom said no, or when your brother hits you and you want to hit him back.

Don't try talking yourself out of it. Get out of there. Tell your parents what you are struggling to do and ask them to help you, but whatever you do, get away from the tempting situation. Run!

Dear God, give me the wisdom and the courage to leave when I need to get away from temptation.

JULY 23

Membership Privileges

Be like those who through faith and patience will receive what God has promised.

HEBREWS 6:12 NCV

If your family has a membership to a fitness club, then you have privileges to use the basketball court, the gym, or the swimming pool. Being a Christian has privileges too.

God gives us many gifts to enjoy at the right time. You have to be patient and trust that his timing is worth the wait. Being obedient to God is worth the privileges you will receive later.

Dear God, please help me be patient while I wait for your timing.

The Flu

We wait in hope for the LORD;
he is our help and our shield.

PSALM 33:20 NIV

Have you ever had the flu? Your body hurts. You have a fever that makes you feel hot one minute and freezing cold the next. You might be so tired you just want to sleep all day. Did someone try to make you feel better with medicine, soup, or a cold cloth on your forehead?

Waiting for God to answer your prayer is like waiting to get better. You try things that will help, and you hold on to the hope that maybe tomorrow your answer will come. Where God is, there is hope.

Dear God, I choose to be hopeful while I wait for you to answer my prayer.

Sea Anemones

Two people are better off than one,
for they can help each other succeed.

ECCLESIASTES 4:9 NLT

A sea anemone lives on the ocean floor waving its long tentacles back and forth with the waves. Beware of those tentacles because they are poisonous. But the little clownfish isn't bothered by the stinging tentacles. The anemone helps protect the clownfish from predators, and the clownfish drops food scraps for the sea anemone. They are a great team.

Good friends are great to have on your side. Friends make you better. They also make good teammates. God knew what he was doing when he gave you friends.

Dear God, I want to be the kind of friend who helps, supports, and stands by others.

JULY 26

Pay Back

These forty years the LORD your God has been with you, and you have not lacked anything.

DEUTERONOMY 2:7 NIV

For forty years the people of Israel wandered around in the desert. No swimming pools. No air conditioning. No houses. Just tents and a lot of dust and heat. They made a lot of bad choices. But their clothes never wore out, and they never went thirsty or hungry.

God doesn't try to pay you back when you do something wrong. He will correct you, but he wants to turn your heart back to him. He wants to get you on the right path that leads to heaven.

Dear God, thank you that you love me enough to correct me.

JULY 27

Tasty Bites

The words of a gossip are like tasty bits of food.
People like to gobble them up.

Proverbs 18:8 NCV

Gossiping can be like handing out tasty bits of information. It can make you feel important to know things other people don't know. But gossip has the power to hurt people.

God warns that gossip stirs up trouble. It turns into rumors and separates friends instead of making them closer. When you're in a conversation and someone starts to gossip, do your best to stop gossip from spreading.

Dear Lord, please remind me to stop talking if I start to share information that I'm not supposed to share.

Rain and Sunshine

I trust him with all my heart.
He helps me, and my heart is filled with joy.

PSALM 28:7 NLT

Not all days are full of sunshine. Clouds appear and rain falls. Some places get a lot of rain. Rainy days are usually gray and gloomy. The sun is never really gone though. It's just tucked behind the clouds.

At times, it can feel like God is far away. During sad times, it can seem like God is missing. He's not! He's always with you, ready to help. He can fill your gloomy heart with joy.

Dear God, please let me feel you near me when I'm sad. Fill my heart with your joy on gloomy days.

Don't Forget to Smile

Happiness makes a person smile.

Proverbs 15:13 NCV

It's fun to be in a wedding. You get a new dress and probably new shoes. Your hair gets done in a pretty hairstyle. You might get to carry a basket of flower petals to throw before the bride walks down the aisle. Don't forget to put on a big smile for all of the pictures.

Whether you're wearing your comfy old pajamas or a fancy new dress, don't forget to smile. Smiling makes you feel good. It makes those around you feel good too. Look for the good things God gives. Choose to let joy show on your face.

Dear God, thinking about all the ways you have made me happy puts a smile on my face.

No More Darkness

He brought them out of their gloom and darkness.
He broke their chains.

PSALM 107:14 ICB

Looking for something in the dark is difficult. We might bump into things, stub our toes, or get frustrated. It's really hard to see without any light. Light makes all the difference when something is lost.

Living your life without Jesus is like searching for something in the dark. Jesus is light, and he will show you the way. It doesn't make sense to wander around in the dark when you don't have to. As a follower of Jesus, you get to walk in the light.

God, thank you for saving me from darkness
and showing me the right way to live.

Seashells

I praise you because I am fearfully and wonderfully made; your works are wonderful.

PSALM 139:14 NIV

People love to walk along ocean beaches and hunt for beautiful shells. There are clam shells and tulip shells, sand dollars and big conch shells. They come in different colors, shapes, and sizes, just like people.

God created so many different kinds of people all around the world. People with red hair, brown eyes, freckly skin. He made tall people and short people. Some people love to laugh, and others like to think. Some love to talk, and some prefer to listen. God made you beautifully *you*.

Dear God, thanks for making me wonderful in my own special way.

AUGUST

Lord, you will give perfect peace
to those who commit themselves
to be faithful to you.
That's because they trust in you.

Isaiah 26:3 NIRV

Counting Sand

God, your thoughts about me are priceless.
No one can possibly add them all up.
If I could count them,
they would be more than the grains of sand.

PSALM 139:17-18 NIRV

Part of the fun of being at the beach is the sand. It squishes under your toes until your feet are completely buried. It sticks together so you can create a castle.

If you scooped up a handful of sand and tried to count each little piece, could you do it? No way! You can't count all the thoughts God has about you either. He thinks about you all day and night. You are that precious to him.

Dear God, thank you for loving me so much that you think about me often.

AUGUST 2

Funny Mirrors

God created human beings in his image. In the image of God he created them. He created them male and female.

GENESIS 1:27 NCV

It is fun to stand in front of funny mirrors and laugh at how goofy they make you look. The curves in the mirrors change your body into weird shapes.

God created people to look like him on the inside: kind, loving, brave, happy, and confident. When sin came into the world, everything changed. Sin twists what God planned for good into ugliness. Ask God to help you look more like him.

Dear God, help me to be strong and not let sin twist me into something bad.

Deep Sea

You will throw away all our sins
into the deepest part of the sea.

MICAH 7:19 NCV

In the deepest parts of the ocean, there are many things we will never see. Getting to the bottom is tricky—and it's very cold down there!

When you do something that makes God sad, ask for forgiveness. Once he forgives you, it's like he throws your sins into the deep sea never to be seen again. They are out of God's sight and out of his mind.

Dear God, your forgiveness is deeper than the deepest sea. Thank you for throwing away my sin.

Splashes of Joy

Always be joyful because you belong to the Lord. I will say it again. Be joyful!

PHILIPPIANS 4:4 NIRV

When you are in the water with your friends, pretty soon someone will start splashing. The cool water splattering across your face is a fun surprise. It makes you laugh, and a splash war will usually break out.

Joy can splash out of your heart like water splashing on your face. There are so many good things God does for you that bring you joy. Think about some of them now.

Dear Lord, you are so good to me.
You give me lots of reasons to be joyful.

Messing Up

Give praise to the God who is able to keep you from falling into sin. He will bring you into his heavenly glory without any fault. He will bring you there with great joy.

JUDE 1:24 NIRV

It is easy to slip and stumble or trip and fall. This Bible verse is talking about falling into sin. A quick, unkind word can hurt feelings. An angry look can spread anger.

Jesus can keep you from slipping, stumbling, and messing up. Before you speak or act, think about what Jesus would say or do. When you follow his example, you can avoid making mistakes.

Dear God, thank you for being patient with me when I mess up.

One-of-a-Kind

We were chosen so that we would bring praise to God's glory.

EPHESIANS 1:12 NCV

You're a special, one-of-a-kind girl who was created to give God glory. You were made to live a good life for him.

When you glorify God in what you do, what you think, and what you say, you are doing what you were created to do.

Dear God, when I do things your way it brings you glory. Teach me to listen to you.

AUGUST 7

Don't Run Away

"While he was still a long way off, his father saw him coming. Filled with love and compassion, he ran to his son, embraced him, and kissed him."

LUKE 15:20 NLT

Once upon a time a man had two sons. One son worked hard and obeyed all the rules. The second son disrespected his dad, took his money, and ran away from home. After he spent all the money, he realized how sorry he was and decided to go back home. He thought his father would be mad at him. But his father was so happy that he ran to hug his son.

You can never do so much wrong that God won't forgive you. If you are sorry and come back to him, he forgives you!

Dear God, thank you for always welcoming me back.

Plans Changed

I have learned how to be content with whatever I have.

PHILIPPIANS 4:11 NLT

It is so disappointing when you have plans that get ruined. Crying about it won't help. Complaining will make others miserable too. Choosing joy isn't easy when you are sad about the way things turned out.

Being thankful can help turn a bad attitude into a better one. Creating a different plan might turn a ruined day into something more fun than you thought. Whatever happens, you can choose to be content.

Dear God, when I get disappointed,
help me to make the best of the situation.

AUGUST 9

Not a Sound

The heavens declare the glory of God;
the skies proclaim the work of his hands.
They have no speech, they use no words;
no sound is heard from them.
Yet their voice goes out into all the earth.

PSALM 19:1, 3-4 NIV

You probably wouldn't come across a talking cactus or praying flowers, and you'll never hear trees that preach. The sun doesn't sing, the moon doesn't make music, and the stars don't shout, but they still praise God through their beauty.

Everything on earth declares that there is a God who created the big world we live in. Listen to the praise of nature.

Dear God, your creation is amazing!
I want to praise you like nature does.

Knock Knock

"Everyone who asks will receive. The one who searches will find. And everyone who knocks will have the door opened."

LUKE 11:10 NCV

Jesus wants us to feel free to ask questions and search for answers. When you pray, it's like knocking on God's door. You can expect him to answer.

It's okay to ask God for what you need and even for what you want. Search for answers in the Bible to the questions you have about God. Keep knocking. Don't give up until you get an answer.

Dear God, thank you for opening the door every time I knock.

AUGUST 11

Waves in the Sea

When you ask God, you must believe and not doubt. Anyone who doubts is like a wave in the sea, blown up and down by the wind.

JAMES 1:6 NCV

Sometimes when you need to make an important choice, it feels like all the thoughts in your brain are swirling around like waves in a stormy sea. It might not seem like a big decision to anyone else, but it does to you.

Ask God for wisdom and believe that he will answer. Trust what you feel him tell you to do and don't give doubt any space in your brain.

Dear God, please give me wisdom
for the choices I need to make.

AUGUST 12

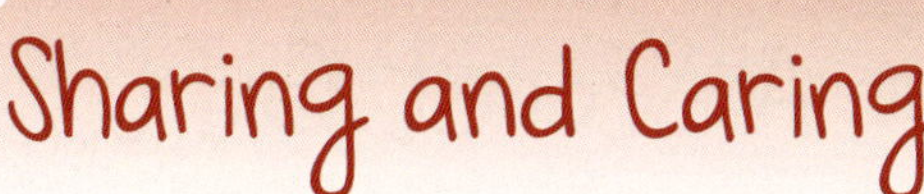

They share freely and give generously to those in need.
Their good deeds will be remembered forever.

Psalm 112:9 NLT

Does your family donate things like clothes and furniture to charity stores? God blesses those who care about the poor. When you give generously, your good deeds will be remembered.

Ask God what he wants you to give. Is it money? Clothes or toys? Pray over the items before you give them away and ask God to bless the person who receives them.

Dear God, thank you that I can bless others
with what you've given me.

A Secret Gift

A secret gift will calm an angry person.

Proverbs 21:14 NCV

Anger can build up inside people like water against a dam, pushing and pushing until the dam bursts. You might not even know that someone is mad at you until they explode. Other times it might be obvious.

Being nice is helpful in a tense situation. Giving a simple gift like a card or flowers or even a hug can make someone feel a little less angry.

Dear God, when someone around me is angry, remind me that giving the gift of kindness can be calming.

AUGUST 14

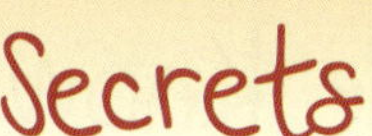

Secrets

God would have known if we had.
He knows what is in our hearts.

PSALM 44:21 ICB

Are you good at keeping a secret? You know that your neighbor is getting a puppy in a week, but it's a secret. You know that your mom bought your dad a new shirt for his birthday, but it's a secret. Are there secrets you shouldn't keep?

If keeping a secret means someone might get hurt, find an adult you trust and let them know. It is more important to keep people from getting hurt than keeping a secret. Be wise with your secrets and know there is nothing hidden from God.

Dear God, help me to be wise with what I keep a secret and what I don't.

AUGUST 15

He Knows

Lord, you have examined my heart
and know everything about me.

Psalm 139:1 NLT

Sometimes reading the Bible seems more about someone else than it does about you. It's God's whole story, but where do you fit in?

The book of Psalms reminds you that God is personal. He knows you. He knows the thoughts in your mind. The psalms are also great to use as prayers when you're not sure what to pray. What is in your heart that you can share with God?

Dear Lord, there's nothing you don't see and nothing you don't know. Help me understand how the stories in the Bible can help me.

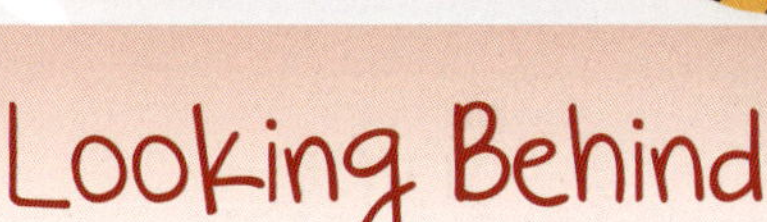

Looking Behind

"I know what you do. I know about your love, your faith, your service, and your patience. I know that you are doing more now than you did at first."

REVELATION 2:19 ICB

Working toward a goal can be hard work. When your goal is still a long way off, looking back can be encouraging. It shows you how far you've come.

Maybe you're saving for something. Keep counting what you have saved and make a money chart to see how close you are getting toward your goal. It is helpful to look back and see how far you've come.

Dear God, thank you for giving me goals and helping me stay focused on reaching those goals.

Shine

"Let your light shine before others, that they may see your good deeds and glorify your Father in heaven."

MATTHEW 5:16 NIV

Some thunderstorms can be strong enough to blow down trees and power lines. If the electricity goes out and you are stuck sitting in total darkness, it can be scary. You need a flashlight or a candle to shine some light so everyone can see.

When you help your parents around the house or offer to play with little kids to give their mom a break, or tell someone about Jesus, you're shining for him. The point of doing good deeds isn't to show people how wonderful you are; it's to point to Jesus.

Dear God, thank you for using me to be a light. Show different ways that I can do good deeds for others.

AUGUST 18

Control Yourself

A gentle answer will calm a person's anger,
but an unkind answer will cause more anger.

PROVERBS 15:1 NCV

It is hard not to say angry words when someone calls you stupid. How do arguments start anyway? Whether you did something on purpose or by accident, don't make the situation worse by joining in and saying angry words back.

Take a breath and ask God to help you control yourself. Use gentleness. Be honest. Admit what you did wrong and apologize for your part. You might need to give someone space and time to cool off. Talk to God about what you can do better next time.

Dear God, remind me to give a gentle answer
when I am angry.

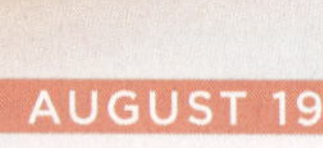

Trusted

"Whoever can be trusted with a little can also be trusted with a lot, and whoever is dishonest with a little is dishonest with a lot."

LUKE 16:10 NCV

Some people are unreliable. They don't put important dates in their calendar. They make promises and don't always follow through. They don't keep a secret. You don't know if you can trust them to make good choices, or to be honest, or to do what they say they'll do.

Trust is a big deal. Be the kind of person people can count on even in the little things. Later you will be trusted with a lot more.

Dear God, help me to be trustworthy and honest.

Words Like Honey

Pleasant words are like a honeycomb.
They make a person happy and healthy.

PROVERBS 16:24 ICB

Pleasant words are full of sweetness. They are wonderful to hear. You can be encouraged and inspired to do good things by someone's sweet words. Complaining is the opposite. It sounds awful. It doesn't change anything. It doesn't make you feel better. Nobody enjoys listening to it.

Your words are powerful, and you need to think carefully before you speak. Try to use your words to help others and not hurt them.

Dear God, you are so good to me. I want my words to be pleasant and sweet like honey to those I talk to.

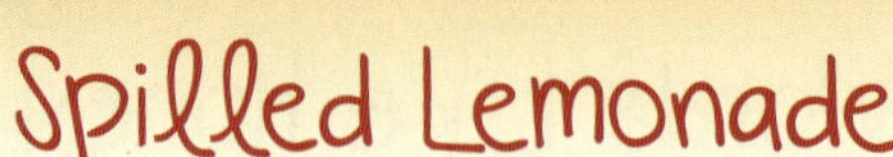

Spilled Lemonade

Trust in him at all times, you people;
pour out your hearts to him,
for God is our refuge.

PSALM 62:8 NIV

Imagine if you spilled lemonade on the kitchen floor while you tried to pour yourself a glass. Then imagine your dad running into the kitchen to help you. He asks if you are ok and makes sure you didn't get hurt. Then he helps you clean up and even pours you a new glass of lemonade.

God is like that. He is ready to help you. You can trust him.

Dear God, thank you that you care about how I feel.
I know you are a safe place for me.

Liar Liar

The snake was the most clever of all the wild animals the LORD God had made. One day the snake said to the woman, "Did God really say that you must not eat fruit from any tree in the garden?"

GENESIS 3:1 NCV

Satan is a clever enemy. He loves to put bad thoughts into your mind to make you doubt what God said and who God is. Have you wondered if God really loves you after something bad happened? Do you think God's Word is still true today even though it was written long ago? When you don't get what you prayed for, do you question if God really answers prayer?

Don't fall for Satan's tricks and lies like Eve did. He is a liar.

Dear God, I know you are good, and Satan is a liar. Help me not to fall for his tricks.

AUGUST 23

Star Light Star Bright

The sky was made at the Lord's command.
By the breath from his mouth, he made all the stars.

Psalm 33:6 ICB

God is so powerful that he made billions of stars appear just by his words. He breathed out of his mouth and each living thing was created. Isn't that amazing?

That is the power of the God you serve. There's nothing he can't do. He can turn a tough situation into something good. He can soften an angry heart. He will give you what you need. Take a few big breaths and thank God for making you.

Dear God, there's nothing you can't do.
Thank you for giving me life.

He Will Help

"I will not fail you or abandon you. Be strong and courageous."

JOSHUA 1:6 NLT

When you are a kid, your parents help teach you how to make good decisions. They remind you of when piano practice is and ask if you got your homework done on time.

God says he will be with you. He uses your parents to help when you are growing up, and he will help you too. Be brave. God is with you.

Dear God, sometimes I feel nervous about all the things that are happening. Please help me to be brave.

The Plan

My child, listen and accept what I say.
I am guiding you in the way of wisdom,
and I am leading you on the right path.

PROVERBS 4:10-11 NCV

You won't always know what God has in mind when he tells you to do something. He may ask you to take steps without understanding the plan, and it might not make sense, or maybe you'd rather do something else.

God is full of surprises, but you can trust that he will lead you on the right path.

Dear God, thank you that I can trust you
to lead me on the right path.

The Hand Off

Commit to the LORD whatever you do,
and he will establish your plans.

PROVERBS 16:3 NIV

In a relay race, runners each take turns running as fast as they can. The first person carries a baton and sprints to the next runner. Then she hands off the baton, and that runner takes it from there. Once that first runner hands off the baton, it's not hers to worry about anymore.

You can think of prayer being like a relay race. You bring your requests to God and then hand them off. He takes it from there, so you don't have to worry about it. Do your part and let God do his.

Dear God, help me to hand off my worries to you.
I trust you to do your part.

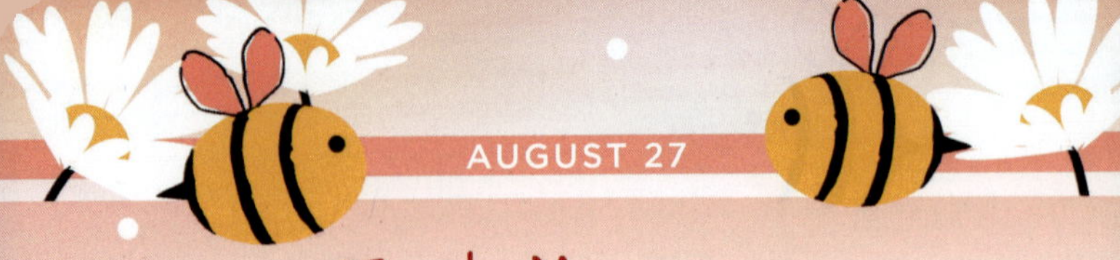

Text Message

Give all your worries to him, because he cares about you.

1 Peter 5:7 NCV

What if you could talk to God by sending him a text message? You could tell him what you are worried about. Then he could reply, and you would know exactly what his answer is for you. That would be so great!

God will respond to you; it's just a little different than getting a text. Tell God about your worries, and then wait and see how he answers. Don't doubt that he cares about you!

Dear God, when I am worried,
help me to come to you for peace.

Under the Sea

LORD, you have made many things.
Look at the sea, so big and wide,
with creatures large and small that cannot be counted.

PSALM 104:24-25 NCV

Some people love to snorkel in the ocean and swim around looking at all the sea creatures. There is a big, wide world under the sea to explore. God filled the sea with many marvelous creatures. Each colorful, slippery, slimy, amazing creature was created uniquely.

Nothing God created was an accident. He knew what he was doing when he made the big sea and the many things that live in it. What a wonderful Creator he is.

Dear God, thank you for the wonder of your creation.

Rich Girl

The LORD is gracious and compassionate,
slow to anger and rich in love.

PSALM 145:8 NIV

If someone is rich, they might have fancy cars, nice clothes, a big house with a pool, and maybe they go on lots of vacations.

Do you think God is rich? He owns everything in heaven and on earth. But he is also rich in love. His love never runs out. He has enough for everyone and will still have leftovers.

Dear God, you make me feel like a rich girl who has everything I need and more because of your love.

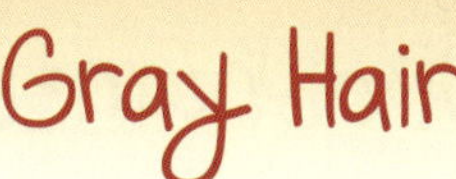

AUGUST 30

Gray Hair

Gray hair is like a crown of honor;
it is earned by living a good life.

PROVERBS 16:31 NCV

Do you like talking to older people? You might wonder if you have anything in common with them. Ask your older family members to tell you about when they were your age. Older people have lived a long time and have lots of good stories and advice.

The next time you are with older people, ask them a question. Find out more about them. See them like Jesus does.

Dear God, help me to learn from people
who are older and wiser than I am.

Unashamed

"If anyone stands before other people and says he believes in me, then I will say that he belongs to me. I will say this before my Father in heaven."

MATTHEW 10:32 ICB

Imagine if a famous singer walked into your school and you got to meet her. What if she walked up, gave you a hug, and then told everyone that you were her friend, and she thinks you are amazing? You would feel pretty important.

If you belong to Jesus, when you get to heaven, he will welcome you in and say that he knows you. Do you tell others about him? He is excited to tell all of heaven that you are his friend.

Dear Jesus, thank you for loving me and not being ashamed of me. Help me to be bold about you too.

SEPTEMBER
Those people who
go to the Lord for help
will have every good thing.
PSALM 34:10 ICB

New Mercy

The LORD's love never ends;
his mercies never stop.
They are new every morning.
LAMENTATIONS 3:23 NCV

God wants you to know that his mercy is new every morning. Each day is a fresh start to try again. It is as if God hands you a new, blank notebook that has none of your mistakes written in it.

He is faithful to keep his promise. He will not remember your sin once you have said sorry and turned away from it. Every day begins with the hope that it is going to be new, different, and better.

Dear God, thank you for being faithful
and giving me mercy when I mess up.

All Kinds of Work

"The Lord has given Bezalel the skill, ability and knowledge to do all kinds of work."

EXODUS 35:31 ICB

God chose a man named Bezalel to make special items out of gold, silver, bronze, jewels, and wood for the place where the Israelites worshiped God. God filled him up with all kinds of skills as an artist, so he was able to make beautiful designs.

God gives some people special creative gifts. Whatever skills God gives you are important because he has special plans for you to use them.

Dear Father, thank you for the skills I need to do a good job.

Better Together

Be joyful with those who are joyful. Be sad with those who are sad. Agree with one another.

ROMANS 12:15-16 NIRV

Be happy for someone when they share good news with you. Don't allow one moment of jealousy to stir up bad feelings. Be a friend who thinks about what is good for others. Don't think about yourself first.

Listen to your friend when she is feeling sad too. Do something to show her you care. Life is much better when you go through things together.

Dear God, thank you for my family and friends. Life without them wouldn't be as good.

Others First

Don't be selfish; don't try to impress others. Be humble, thinking of others as better than yourselves.

PHILIPPIANS 2:3 NLT

Instead of only thinking about what you want, look at the other people in your life. Do your brothers and sisters need help with their chores? Can you share your lunch with someone who forgot theirs? Would you let your neighbor go first on the swing?

Jesus always put others first. He healed people because he cared about them. He gave up his life so you could be in his family. If you love Jesus, follow his example of loving people.

Dear Jesus, help me to stop selfish thoughts and think about how I can help others instead.

Be Still

"Be still and know that I am God.
I will be praised in all the nations;
I will be praised throughout the earth."

PSALM 46:10 NCV

Is it hard for you to sit still? Do you feel wiggly? Some people fidget with their hands, play with their hair, or bite their nails. Usually, when you can't sit still it's because you don't feel still on the inside.

God can help you be quiet on the inside. He is in control. He knows what's going on. He sees everything. He is powerful, and he hears your prayers. Talk to God and then be still.

Dear God, please quiet my heart with your peace.
You are a big, powerful God.

September 6

Mirror Mirror

Those who hear God's teaching and do nothing are like people who look at themselves in a mirror. They see their faces and then go away and quickly forget what they looked like.

James 1:23-24 NCV

If you look in a mirror, and something's on your face, you clean it off. It would be silly to leave it there.

Listening to God's Word without doing what it says is like leaving that mark on your face. Don't ignore what God is telling you to do. Be smart and obey.

Dear God, help me to put what I learn about you into action.

SEPTEMBER 7

Sabbath

"You have six days each week for your ordinary work,
but the seventh day must be a Sabbath day of complete rest,
a holy day dedicated to the LORD."

EXODUS 31:15 NLT

God knew that people would need a day to rest. He created the Sabbath day as a day to stop doing work. You need rest for your body and mind. Take a break from the all the things that distract you from God.

Think of ways you can rest. Go on a walk, swing in a hammock, find a quiet reading spot, or get cozy by the fire. Think about what you learned at church. Talk to God and let him bring you rest.

Dear Lord, help me to rest, reflect,
and get refreshed by you on the Sabbath.

Happy or Guilty

Happy is the person
whom the LORD does not consider guilty
and in whom there is nothing false.

PSALM 32:2 NCV

God blesses those who are honest with happiness. Guilt is a very yucky feeling that God doesn't want you to have. He is good, so he wants good things for you.

If you are guilty of doing something wrong, make it right. Ask God for forgiveness. Don't blame other people when you make a bad choice. Be honest. Tell the truth. A happy, guilt-free heart is worth the work of doing what is right.

Dear God, I don't want the yucky feeling of guilt.
I want to make you proud of me for being honest.

Choose Carefully

The righteous choose their friends carefully,
but the way of the wicked leads them astray.

PROVERBS 12:26 NIV

It is so important to choose your friends carefully. Friends can help you make good choices. They can also lead you into bad things.

Think about the friends you have right now. Who pleases Jesus in how they behave? Who encourages you to do good things? Do your friends share your faith in Jesus? Decide who would be good friends and keep them close.

God, thank you for good friends.
Help me to choose my friends carefully.

Practice Makes Perfect

"Be perfect, therefore, as your heavenly Father is perfect."

MATTHEW 5:48 NIV

In order to get better at something, you need to practice. You practice piano so that you will play your song without making a mistake. You practice gymnastics so you won't fall. You practice spelling so you can read, and you practice math problems so you will be wise with your money.

Trying your best is great, but practice is also needed. Only God is perfect, but you are encouraged to try to be like him. Ask him to help you.

Dear God, thank you for loving me even though I'm not perfect. Help me to be like you.

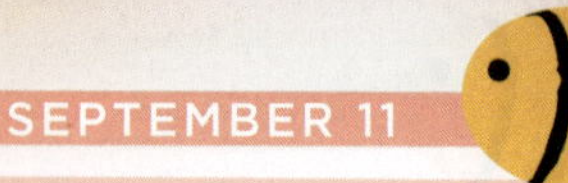

Use Your Head

Trust the Lord with all your heart.
Don't depend on your own understanding.

PROVERBS 3:5 ICB

When you are looking for an answer to what you're praying for, you can ask yourself what makes the most sense, but don't just depend on your own thoughts. Check with a few adults you can trust.

God answers prayers in many ways. Write down and remember how God has answered your prayers. You will see that you can trust him.

Dear God, please make me wise and help me use my head to make good decisions.

Good Advice

The wisdom that comes from God is first of all pure, then peaceful, gentle, and easy to please. This wisdom is always ready to help those who are troubled and to do good for others. It is always fair and honest.

JAMES 3:17 NCV

When someone gives you advice, how do you know if it is good? They might be really smart or know you better than anyone else, but that's not enough. It's not that easy.

Wisdom from God is pure and gentle. It chooses what is fair and honest. It brings you peace, and it helps other people. If this is the advice you get, take it. Real wisdom will lead to good results.

Dear God, thank you for showing me how to decide if the advice I get is good or bad.

I Can Do It

I can do everything through Christ, who gives me strength.

PHILIPPIANS 4:13 NLT

God gives you strength to push situations that are difficult. You might be disappointed or frustrated about something, or you might not get exactly what you want. There will be times when you have to be ok with what you already have.

What do you need to be content with right now? Ask God for strength to be content with what you have and not fuss about wanting more.

Dear God, thank you for giving me strength to be content.

Hurt Feelings

He comforts us every time we have trouble, so when others have trouble, we can comfort them with the same comfort God gives us.

2 Corinthians 1:4 NCV

God made our bodies to feel pain when we get hurt. Sometimes we hurt on the inside. We can have hurt feelings from angry words. We can feel embarrassed by mistakes. We can feel left out, lonely, and sad. People don't always see those hurts, and they might be hard to talk about.

You don't have to come up with the right words to explain how you feel to God. He understands. He is always with you, ready to help take some of the hurt away.

Dear God, thank you for seeing my hurt and understanding me.

Me First

Be devoted to one another in love. Honor one another above yourselves.

ROMANS 12:10 NIV

As a follower of Jesus, you are supposed to put others before yourself. You let them go first. When an opportunity comes up, ask God what you should do. You probably already know the answer in your heart.

Do what God tells you to do. You do your part and trust God will take care of the rest. When you care for others before yourself, it makes God happy.

Dear God, help me to trust that when you ask me to put others first, you will still take care of me.

Walk the Dog

We take captive every thought to make it obedient to Christ.

2 Corinthians 10:5 NIV

Walking a dog can feel like you are being pulled this way and that, over here, over there, stop, go. Sometimes your thoughts can be like that. Good and bad thoughts swirl around in your brain. When negative thoughts come in, it's time to pull on the leash and get those bad thoughts under control.

Recognize what is a bad thought and stop it from running around in your mind. Make those bad thoughts obedient to Christ by thinking of what Jesus would do instead. You can be a strong girl who takes control of her thoughts.

Dear God, teach me to recognize bad thoughts right away and make them obedient to you.

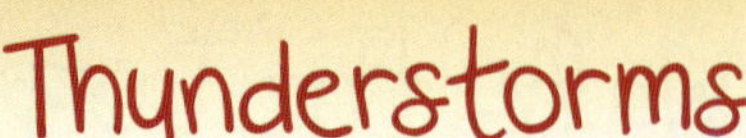

Thunderstorms

We will not fear though the earth give way
and the mountains fall into the heart of the sea,
though its waters roar and foam
and the mountains quake with their surging.

Psalm 46:2-3 NIV

Thunderstorms can be loud and scary. Watching a storm roll by can be interesting when you are sitting safe inside. Having someone older right beside you and being able to talk about the storm can make you feel better.

Even when there are storms, tornados, fires, earthquakes, and flooding, God says not to fear. He is always close. You can face the storm clouds with him and not be afraid.

Dear God, no matter what happens,
you are always with me.

The Perfect Pick

"Saul has stopped following me. And I am sorry I made him king. He has not obeyed my commands."

1 SAMUEL 15:11 ICB

King Saul seemed like the perfect pick for a king, but then he chose to turn away from God. A new king was needed, so God sent the prophet Samuel out on a mission. God told Samuel not to pick someone based on how he looked on the outside. God chose David because he had a heart that loved and obeyed God.

Do you love God and spend time talking to him? Do you treat other people with kindness? Keep your heart turned toward God and never stop trying to obey him.

Dear God, show me what matters most to you, so I can be like that.

SEPTEMBER 19

Corn Maze

How great are God's riches and wisdom and knowledge! How impossible it is for us to understand his decisions and his ways!

ROMANS 11:33 NLT

During the fall when leaves turn colors, there are festivals with pumpkins, apple picking, hayrides, and corn mazes. People follow different paths through ten-foot cornstalks trying to find the way out. It's tricky but fun.

Sometimes life is like a maze. You don't know which way to go. You won't always be able to figure everything out or understand what's going on. God knows and he understands even when you can't.

Dear God, you know everything, so I can trust you to help me out of any situation.

Okay with Ordinary

Don't you know that you are God's temple and that God's Spirit lives in you?

1 CORINTHIANS 3:16 NCV

Average. Regular. Ordinary. That describes most people. They blend in. Do you feel like you disappear in a group of people, and no one really knows you are there? Jesus understands that. The Bible says there was nothing about Jesus that made people notice him even though he was the Son of God.

You might be ordinary, but there is something special about you if you have asked Jesus into your heart. You are God's holy temple, and his power lives in you.

Dear God, thank you for living in me and giving me strength.

Better Than

As believers in our glorious Lord Jesus Christ, never think some people are more important than others.

JAMES 2:1 NCV

If one of your friends lived in a big, beautiful house, would you treat her better than a friend who lived in a small apartment?

God does not agree with treating some people better than others. One person isn't more important than another person. Everyone is important and should be treated with love and kindness.

Dear God, help me to be fair in how I treat my friends. Teach me how to love like Jesus.

SEPTEMBER 22

Do Over

"When you offer your gift to God at the altar, and you remember that your brother or sister has something against you, leave your gift there at the altar. Go and make peace with that person, and then come and offer your gift."

MATTHEW 5:23-24 NCV

Sometimes you just need a do over. Maybe you said something mean and hurt your friend's feelings. You might have gotten mad and pushed your sister or talked back to your mom. Then you feel bad. You wish you could go back and do those moments over.

You can't take back what you did, but you can make things right. Go say sorry. Even if they don't forgive you, God will see you tried to make peace.

Dear God, please give me the courage to go and apologize when I'm wrong.

Getting Bullied

Peninnah teased Hannah year after year. Every time Hannah would go up to the house of the LORD, Elkanah's other wife would tease her. She would keep doing it until Hannah cried and wouldn't eat.

1 SAMUEL 1:6-7 NIRV

Hannah knew what it was like to be teased. She would get so upset that she would cry and didn't feel like eating. What a terrible bully the other woman was to poor Hannah.

Hannah prayed to God, and he heard her. He answered her prayers. Have you been bullied, or do you know someone who has? Tell God how you feel. He will always hear you.

Dear God, thank you for hearing me.
When I am bullied, show me what to do.

Loving and Liking

"Love your enemies, do good to them."

LUKE 6:35 NIV

You don't have to like someone to love them. Liking someone means you enjoy spending time with them, you have fun together, and they make you feel good when you're around them. Loving means treating someone the way Jesus would treat them even if they don't treat you well.

Love is choosing to do what's right. Loving your enemies means praying for them and doing good without expecting anything back. You can love without liking.

Dear God, some people are hard to love. Remind me to do good to them whether I feel like it or not.

SEPTEMBER 25

Different

You created my inmost being;
you knit me together in my mother's womb.

Psalm 139:13 NIV

When people look, sound, or act differently, you might not be sure what to do. Be friendly. They have feelings too. Don't talk to them rudely. Don't stare, but don't ignore them either. Smile at them.

Be kind and treat people how you want to be treated. God loves the people he has created in his own special way.

Dear God, help me to treat people who are different than me with kindness.

In Jesus' Name

"The nations will put their hope in him."

MATTHEW 12:21 NIRV

The name of Jesus means more than a name like Jacob or Sam or Peter. It stands for everything Jesus is and everything he has done. Maybe you were taught to end your prayer saying, "in Jesus' name." You are recognizing the power in the name of Jesus.

Jesus has power over death. He can forgive your sin. Calling on Jesus' name and praying in that same name makes things happen.

Dear Jesus, thank you for the power of your name.
I pray boldly in your name.

SEPTEMBER 27

Money Money Money

"Store your treasure in heaven. The treasures in heaven cannot be destroyed by moths or rust. And thieves cannot break in and steal that treasure."

MATTHEW 6:20 ICB

Jesus said that those who are rich can have hard time following God. But having lots of money can also be a gift for you and for those you share your money with.

Whether you have a lot or a little, share your gift in a way that pleases God. God says to be generous. He loves a cheerful giver. Be fair. Give people what you owe them. Don't be selfish. When you see someone in need, help them. Be generous and store up your treasure in heaven.

Dear God, help me to guard my heart so I don't let money become more important than you.

Woven Together

We know that God causes everything to work together for the good of those who love God and are called according to his purpose for them.

ROMANS 8:28 NLT

God uses everything that happens in your life to create a beautiful design. There are happy days and sad days and some boring days in between. He takes it all and makes it part of your story.

You can only see a little piece of your life so far, and it might not seem like much. When Jesus comes back, everything will make sense. You will be able to see the whole pattern and God's beautiful design for your life.

Dear God, thank you that you can use everything in my life and make it work out for good.

Bad Company

Don't let anyone fool you. "Bad companions make a good person bad."

1 Corinthians 15:33 NIRV

You might feel uncomfortable around kids that make bad choices, but if you continue to hang out with them, you will start to act like them. The more you are with them, the more you become like them whether you mean to or not.

If the kids you are around do bad stuff, make bad choices or talk bad, it is time to stop hanging out with them. When you choose friends, pick people who will encourage you to be more like Jesus.

Dear God, help me to choose good friends and help me to be a good friend.

Move Over

"Love your neighbor as you love yourself." If you obey this law, you are doing right.

James 2:8 NCV

How do you love others like you love yourself? When you are filled with God's love, you will want to do things for others that you would usually want to do for yourself.

You are loved by God, and you know God loves other people as much as he loves you. Think of some ways you can love your neighbor as you love yourself right now.

Dear God, help me come up with some good ideas on how to show love to the people around me.

OCTOBER

"In repentance and rest is your salvation,
in quietness and trust is your strength."

Isaiah 30:15 NIV

Apples

We all have different gifts. Each gift came because of the grace that God gave us.

Romans 12:6 ICB

Apples make good snacks. Some are perfect for pies and baking. Others are great for dipping in caramel sauce or making into juice. Each apple can be used in different ways.

God gave each person different gifts sort of like the different apples. One gift isn't better than the other. They are just used for different things. Work together with the believers around you and use whatever your gift is to cheerfully help one another.

Dear God, show me what gift you have for me and how to use it well.

OCTOBER 2

Good Different

By faith Abraham, when called to go to a place he would later receive as his inheritance, obeyed and went, even though he did not know where he was going.

HEBREWS 11:8 NIV

Would you be willing to try something different or do you prefer to do things the same way you usually do? *Different* isn't always bad. Sometimes it can be good.

You might not have to walk through something as big as moving to a place far away. Maybe it's something small like trying a new food or doing something you've never done before. Whatever different thing you face, don't assume it will be bad. Give it a try.

Dear God, I feel comfortable with what's familiar. Give me the courage to try what's different.

OCTOBER 3

Two or Three

"Where two or three gather in my name, there am I with them."

MATTHEW 18:20 NIV

When two or more people who believe in Jesus get together, God's Spirit is with them. Whether you are worshipping at church, sharing stories of God's goodness around a bonfire, hiking together on a nature trail, or praying at bedtime, God is there with you.

Remember this the next time you get together to pray.

Dear God, thank you I am able to pray, worship, and hang out with other people who love you. Thank you that you are there.

My Own Fault

Heavens and earth, be happy.
Mountains, shout with joy.
Be happy because the Lord comforts his people.

ISAIAH 49:13 ICB

The people of Israel got into trouble over and over when they decided to do what they wanted when they wanted. God still loved them even though they kept messing up. Have you ever gotten into trouble, and it was your own fault? Sometimes there are big consequences for the mistakes you make.

God still has compassion on you. He is there to comfort you just like he did for the people of Israel. Tell God how thankful you are for his comfort and compassion.

Dear God, thank you for having compassion even if it's my own fault that I got myself in a mess.

OCTOBER 5

Give your burdens to the Lord,
and he will take care of you.

Psalm 55:22 NLT

Prayer is taking your burdens, worries, and hurt feelings to God. You hand them over because you know he will take care of you. You let him handle whatever you've prayed about. You don't go back to worrying.

Once you pray and tell God what's bothering you, leave it with God and trust that he will take care of you.

Dear God, when something is bothering me,
remind me to go to you and then leave it there.

Daughter of God

You are all children of God through faith in Christ Jesus.

GALATIANS 3:26 ICB

The Bible says that you are a daughter of God. You are part of his family. If you have faith in Jesus and have asked him into your heart, then he calls you his own.

You are God's girl, and he wants the whole world to know you are his. Don't ever believe a lie saying you are something you are not. You are a daughter of the King!

Dear Jesus, thank you for making me part of your family.

OCTOBER 7

Shadows

Every good and perfect gift is from above, coming down from the Father of the heavenly lights, who does not change like shifting shadows.

JAMES 1:17 NIV

Shadows move and change, depending on how the sun shines. You can move one way, and your shadow will look different. Thankfully God is not like that. He never changes from who he really is. He is always faithful and trustworthy.

Sometimes things happen that might make you think God has changed, but he hasn't changed at all. When you don't understand, remind yourself of what you know. God is good. He is perfect. And he does not change.

Dear God, you always do what you say you'll do. Thank you for keeping your promises.

Bad Day

Job had three friends. They heard about all the troubles that had come to Job. So they started out from their homes. They had agreed to meet together. They wanted to go and show their concern for Job. They wanted to comfort him.

JOB 2:11 NIRV

There is a book in the Bible named after the man, Job, who had a terrible day. In one day, Job lost everything he had: all his animals and crops, his house and servants, and all his children.

Job's friends heard the news and came to comfort him.

When they arrived and saw their friend, do you know what they said to him? Nothing. Sometimes just being there for your friend is enough. Sometimes words won't help. You can still show love and comfort by being silent.

Dear God, when my friends need to be comforted, help me know what to do.

Really Known

LORD, you have seen what is in my heart.
You know all about me.

PSALM 139:2 NIRV

One day, after all the other women went inside, a lonely lady headed out to fetch water. No one wanted to be her friend because she had made bad choices. They whispered behind her back and called her names. She was embarrassed to be around people, so she went to the well alone.

Jesus was there waiting for her. He was kind to her. He talked to her. He knew all about her.

He told her about his gift of eternal life. Just like Jesus knew that lonely lady, he knows all about you, and he loves you.

Dear Jesus, you know everything about me,
and you still love me.

OCTOBER 10

Super Slow

You are a God who forgives. You are gracious. You are tender and kind. You are slow to get angry. You are full of love.

NEHEMIAH 9:17 NIRV

Have you ever tried to get honey from the bottom of the jar and waited and waited for it to slowly slide out? It is a slow process especially when you're hungry.

There is one thing that God is really slow at—getting angry. He is full of compassion. He loves you. He always wants to give you another chance to make good choices.

Dear God, thank you for being slow to anger and patient with me. I love you.

Gentle and Quiet

Your beauty should come from within you—the beauty of a gentle and quiet spirit that will never be destroyed and is very precious to God.

1 PETER 3:4 NCV

What does it really mean to have a gentle and quiet spirit? It doesn't mean you can't speak up or share your thoughts and ideas. Or that you have to always be quiet.

It means you carefully choose words to say that are kind, not hurtful. You don't get angry easily. You pause and take a breath. You share your thoughts and feelings in a respectful way without interrupting others.

Dear God, teach me to speak kind, encouraging words.

Beautifully Dressed

"Look at how the lilies in the field grow. They don't work or make clothes for themselves. But I tell you that even Solomon with his riches was not dressed as beautifully as one of these flowers."

MATTHEW 6:28-29 NCV

Tulips are so famous in Holland that there are tulip tours, tulip festivals, tulip flower markets, and even a tulip museum. You can even buy tulip bulbs in the Holland airport to bring home on the plane with you.

Tulips, like lilies and roses, come in all different colors. Jesus said that not even King Solomon, one of the richest kings in history, was dressed as beautifully as a flower. If God takes care of the flowers, then of course he will take care of you.

Dear God, thank you for creating beautiful flowers and for caring about me the most.

Tumbling Around

I must find my rest in God.
He is the God who gives me hope.

PSALM 62:5 NIRV

When you throw clothes in the washing machine, they tumble back and forth, upside down, around and around. That's how life can feel too sometimes. Do you ever want to jump into bed, close your eyes, and skip all the activities.

When that happens, there are ways to help you feel better. Go for a walk. Listen to worship music. Go for a bike ride. Spend time with a friend. Most importantly, rest in God. Go to him and pray about what is bothering you.

Dear God, thank you for being my safe place where I can rest.

I'm Not Wrong

Anyone who loves learning accepts correction,
but a person who hates being corrected is stupid.

PROVERBS 12:1 NCV

How do you feel when someone tells you that you're wrong? Instead of getting mad, listen. Admit you don't know everything. Your parents, teachers, and coaches are trying to help make you better.

Being able to accept correction makes you strong mentally and emotionally. Thank the people in your life who are trying to help you learn.

Dear Father, teach me to listen to correction.
Thank you for putting people in my life who care.

OCTOBER 15

Celebrating Awesome

Come, everyone! Clap your hands!
Shout to God with joyful praise!
For the LORD Most High is awesome.
He is the great King of all the earth.

PSALM 47:1-2 NLT

Clapping and shouting joyfully can be loud! It's good to be excited about how awesome God is, and to celebrate that with lots of energy. What if you worshipped God at church like this?

When you realize how big, awesome, wonderful, good, and powerful God is, you can't help but celebrate. Close the door, turn up the worship music, sing, dance, and praise the Lord!

Dear Lord, you are the great King of all the earth.
I praise you because you are awesome.

Voices

The LORD says, "Don't be afraid of what you have heard. Don't be frightened by the words the servants of the king of Assyria have spoken against me."

ISAIAH 37:6 NCV

Things did not look good for King Hezekiah. The city was surrounded. They were trapped and afraid. The enemy started to shout at them. Do you ever hear voices in your mind or the voices of other people trying to make you doubt what you've been told?

If you have thoughts pop into your head that don't sound right, remember that God says not to be afraid. Trust him. He has a plan. Listen to him.

Dear God, I am sometimes confused by people saying different things. Help me ignore those voices and just listen to you.

Mighty Warrior

The angel of the Lord appeared to Gideon and said,
"The Lord is with you, mighty warrior!"

Judges 6:12 NCV

The Israelites stopped obeying the Lord and their enemies kept attacking them. For years, the enemies would eat their food, steal their animals, and destroy their crops. Gideon was hiding when an angel appeared and called him a mighty warrior. Gideon didn't feel strong at all. He became braver as he obeyed God.

When God looks at you, he sees all the possibilities you have. You don't have to be perfect. You just need to be willing to obey and follow God.

Dear God, help me to trust you with all my heart so you can do mighty things in my life.

With All I Am

Let all that I am praise the LORD;
may I never forget the good things he does for me.

PSALM 103:2 NLT

What do you like about God? Tell him. That's called praise. He loves to hear what you think is so amazing about him. There are many reasons why God deserves praise. Can you think of two or three things?

Never forget the good things God does for you. He forgives all your sins and heals you. He fills your life with good things and good people. Praise him today.

Dear God, I praise you because you are so good.

Real Love

Love never fails.

1 CORINTHIANS 13:8 NIV

Real love comes from God because God is love. Real love is a choice. Feelings can change depending on your mood, but you can choose to love someone even if you don't feel like it. Real love is being patient, kind, and believing the best of someone else.

People who love help those in need. They forgive and pray for their enemies. They give things up for their friends. That is the real love of God.

Dear Jesus, thank you for showing me what real love is.

Love Is Not

Love is not jealous, it does not brag, and it is not proud. Love is not rude, is not selfish, and does not get upset with others. Love does not count up wrongs that have been done.

1 CORINTHIANS 13:4-5 NCV

The word *love* gets used a lot, and then you can forget what it really means. This verse talks about what love doesn't look like.

Real love doesn't have bad thoughts about someone. It doesn't brag about what you've done or get upset with others and stay mad. Real love isn't happy when something bad happens to someone else. All those things look ugly. Real love makes you look lovely.

Dear God, please show me how
to love others like you love me.

Loving the Unlovable

The Holy Spirit produces this kind of fruit in our lives: love, joy, peace, patience, kindness, goodness, faithfulness, gentleness, and self-control.

GALATIANS 5:22-23 NLT

There are some people who are really hard to love. You know you're supposed to be patient with them, but they talk about themselves so much that you get tired of listening to them. You know you're supposed to be kind, but they can be rude and mean. How do you love someone like that?

You won't be able to be loving on your own, but the Holy Spirit can help you. Make sure there's nothing in your life that keeps the Holy Spirit from working in and through you.

Dear God, I can't love someone difficult on my own. Thank you for helping me.

OCTOBER 22

The Greatest

"'Love the Lord your God with all your heart and with all your soul and with all your mind.' This is the first and greatest commandment."

MATTHEW 22:37-38 NIV

Jesus said the greatest commandment is to love God with all of you. If you took all the rules in the Bible and squished them into one simple command it would be to love God.

Loving God will make all the difference in what you say and what you do. Loving with all your heart, soul, and mind means loving God with everything you've got. It's thinking about him during the day and including him in all areas of your life.

Dear God, I want to love you with everything I've got.

OCTOBER 23

Stop Fear

"The LORD is with us. So don't be afraid of them."

NUMBERS 14:9 NCV

Everyone feels fear. That's normal. What you do with that fear is what matters. When you are faced with fear, you can take control of it instead of letting it control you. Don't let fear stop you from trying something new or standing up to a bully or making new friends.

You know God is in control and that he is always with you. You are never alone. When you feel afraid, tell the fearful thoughts to be quiet. God will protect you.

Dear God, thank you for always being with me, so I don't have to be afraid of being alone.

What to Say

God, be merciful to me
because you are loving.

Psalm 51:1 NCV

King David had everything he wanted. He had a beautiful palace, many servants, lots of money, and a big family, but David wanted more. David made mistakes and had to ask God for forgiveness. King David wrote this verse to God.

Verses in the Bible can show you how to talk to God when you have a hard time finding your own words. If you need to ask God to forgive you for something you did wrong, you could pray this verse too.

Dear God, thank you for the Bible. It gives me words to pray when I don't know what to say.

Changing Beauty

God is not a human being, and he will not lie.
He is not a human, and he does not change his mind.

NUMBERS 23:19 NCV

What people call beautiful today is very different than it was years ago, and it keeps changing. Beauty is different all around the world.

Beauty in God's kingdom will always remain the same. It doesn't change because God doesn't change. Inner beauty is what's important to God. He sees your heart. He watches how you act and hears how you talk. Be the kind of girl who is beautiful in God's eyes.

Dear God, thank you that you never change.
Help me work on becoming beautiful on the inside.

Words and Thoughts

LORD, may these words of my mouth please you.
And may these thoughts of my heart please you also.

PSALM 19:14 NIRV

Your words should please God and your thoughts too. What you feel on the inside should line up with what you say on the outside, but that's not always easy to do.

Changing negative thoughts into positive thoughts takes practice. So does controlling the words that come out of your mouth. Pause before speaking and ask yourself if what you are about to say or do will please God.

Dear Lord, please help me control my thoughts and my words so that they are pleasing to you.

Lunchtime

"How can we get enough bread to feed all these people? We are far away from any town."

MATTHEW 15:33 NCV

For three days, thousands of people had camped out and listened to Jesus preach. They were far away from any town and the people were getting hungry. The disciples told Jesus the problem. They said what they didn't have, but Jesus asked what they did have. He prayed over the small amount they had. All those people ate until they were full that day.

God doesn't see a problem with what you don't have. He is more powerful than that. He can take what little there is and make miracles happen.

Dear God, teach me to think big, ask big, and believe big because you are a big God.

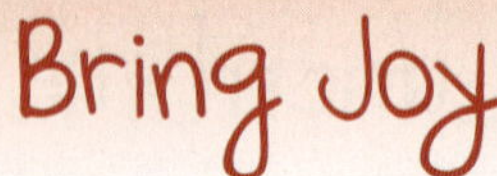

Bring Joy

Obey your leaders and act under their authority. They are watching over you, because they are responsible for your souls. Obey them so that they will do this work with joy, not sadness. It will not help you to make their work hard.

HEBREWS 13:17 NCV

Parents aren't perfect. They make mistakes just like you do. Everyone is responsible to God for what they do. You are not responsible for what anyone else does. You are only responsible for yourself.

Your parents are your leaders. You should obey them and make their job as parents easier. Pray for them. Thank them for working hard to provide for you. Bring joy to your parents.

Dear God, thanks for giving me someone to watch over me. Help me obey and bring them joy.

It's Dark Outside

"You are the light of the world—like a city on a hilltop that cannot be hidden."

MATTHEW 5:14 NLT

You can see a light best in the darkness. If you turn a light on during the day, you will hardly notice the difference. If you light a campfire on a dark night, people can see the light from miles away. Light makes people feel warm and safe.

If you're living for Jesus, you're like a light to the world that is dark with sin. Get out and shine for those who don't know God.

Dear Jesus, you are the light of the world.
Help me to be a light to those who don't know you.

Stand Up

Who will help me fight against the wicked?
Who will stand with me against those who do evil?

PSALM 94:16 ICB

Queen Esther faced a problem that kept her up at night trying to find a solution. She knew she had to stand up to a wicked man, so she approached the king not knowing if she would live or die.

God gave Esther the courage she needed to stand up for God. He can give you courage to stand up for what's right too. Pray about your problem and talk to someone you trust.

Dear God, I don't always have courage.
Please show me how to stand up for what's right.

God Is Family

He is a father to children whose fathers have died.
He takes care of women whose husbands have died.
God gives lonely people a family.

PSALM 68:5-6 NIRV

It is a blessing to have someone to take care of you. Not everyone has that. God says he's a father to the fatherless. He takes care of kids who don't have parents anymore. When someone is lonely, he puts that person in a family.

If you know someone who is missing a dad, mom, or even both, pray for them and ask God what you can do for them.

Dear God, thank you for the family I have. Show me how I can help take care of those who are lonely.

NOVEMBER
You are my hiding place.
You protect me from my troubles.
You fill me with songs of salvation.
PSALM 32:7 ICB

Sweet Tooth

How sweet your words taste to me;
they are sweeter than honey.
PSALM 119:103 NLT

When people like sweets, we sometimes say they have a sweet tooth. Would you choose cookies over chips or ice cream over popcorn? Maybe the writer of Psalm 119 had a sweet tooth. He called God's Word sweeter than honey.

God's Word has the power to give you joy, comfort, and wise advice. The Bible isn't just a book with pages of black and white words. The words have meaning and power. They will make your life sweeter.

Dear God, help me understand and love your Word.

Work Hard

Go watch the ants, you lazy person.
Watch what they do and be wise.
PROVERBS 6:6 ICB

When you clear the table, do the dishes, take out the trash, or clean up after yourself without being asked, that pleases your parents and God too.

God uses the ants as an example of working hard. Ants may be small, but they are mighty little creatures. They work, plan, organize, and hustle. Learn from the example of the ants and work hard without someone having to tell you.

Dear God, sometimes I don't feel like doing what I should. Help me to practice working hard.

Thankful for It All

Be thankful in all circumstances, for this is God's will for you who belong to Christ Jesus.

1 Thessalonians 5:18 NLT

What is something you are having a hard time being thankful for? You can be thankful even when you don't understand why something is happening. Being thankful is a choice.

Ask God to change your heart and be thankful even in hard times.

Dear God, help me to choose to be thankful whether I feel like it or not.

Hard to Forgive

Now that their father was dead, Joseph's brothers became fearful. "Now Joseph will show his anger and pay us back for all the wrong we did to him."

GENESIS 50:15 NLT

It is hard to forgive someone who hurt you, especially if they don't say sorry. You still need to forgive them, but that doesn't mean the hurt will go away and you will feel fine.

By forgiving someone, you are not saying what the person did to hurt you was okay. Forgiving means letting go of being angry. Let God take care of it.

Dear God, when someone hurts my feelings, help me let go of my anger and let you deal with it.

NOVEMBER 5

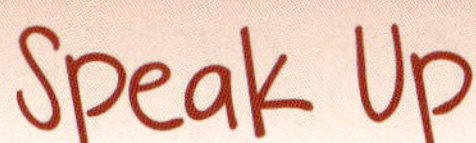

"Speak up for those who cannot speak for themselves; defend the rights of all those who have nothing.

PROVERBS 31:8 NCV

Some things are not okay to see but do nothing about. You can stand up for those who are poor. If you don't know what to do, pray. Ask God what he wants you to do.

Speak up by asking an adult to help, defend someone by telling bullies to stop, raise money for the poor in your community, collect food items or winter clothes, and pray some more.

Dear God, I want to do something for those around me who need help. Show me what to do.

Thank God Every Time

I thank my God every time I remember you.

PHILIPPIANS 1:3 NIV

You have so many things to say thank you for. When someone gives you a gift, does something nice, or says nice things about you, that would be the right time to say thank you.

God puts people in your life who make you feel great. Telling them you are thankful for them will make them feel great too.

Dear God, thank you for amazing people who fill my life with good things.

Whack-a-Mole

The LORD delights in those who fear him,
who put their hope in his unfailing love.

PSALM 147:11 NIV

Ever have one of those days where you sleep in too late and don't have time to eat breakfast? Your stomach makes strange noises, and everyone looks at you. You look down at your socks and realize you have one white and one pink. After school you realize you have soccer practice, and you forgot your gym bag.

Some days you kind of feel like you are the mole in the whack-a-mole game. You keep getting knocked down. Close your eyes and say a quick prayer asking Jesus to help you. He is the answer to turning your day around.

Dear God, I know you love me, and you love to help me. Please turn my bad day around.

No Appointment Needed

Let us come boldly to the throne of our gracious God. There we will receive his mercy, and we will find grace to help us when we need it most.

HEBREWS 4:16 NLT

The Oval Office is the president's office. The only people allowed to go into the Oval Office to see the president have to be invited in, and they go through a lot of strict security steps.

When you need to talk to God, you can go right to him. No appointment is necessary, and no security system will hold you back. You don't need to check in with the Secret Service, go through a metal detector, or wait for an invitation. You can go straight to God and talk to him.

Dear God, even though you are the King of the universe, I can always come to you for help.

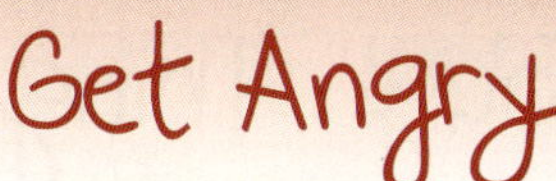

Get Angry

When they came near the camp, Moses saw the calf and the dancing, and he burned with anger.

EXODUS 32:19 NLT

Sometimes it's ok to get angry. After God gave Moses the Ten Commandments, Moses walked down the mountain and saw the Israelites dancing and worshipping a statue of a golden calf. What they were doing was wrong. It was against God's law. It was hurtful to God, and it made Moses angry.

It's okay to be angry when people do something wrong or hurt others on purpose. How you react can make things better or worse. Pray for God to show you what you can do.

Dear God, show me the best way to react when others are doing wrong.

Tough Things

We know and rely on the love God has for us. God is love.

1 John 4:16 NIV

Some things are hard to understand. People get sick with terrible diseases, some families split up, and some parents lose their jobs. Sometimes it just doesn't make sense, and it might even make you angry because you think it's not fair.

There may not be much you can do. Focus on what you know. God is love. What's happening doesn't mean God doesn't love you or doesn't love the person who it's happening to. His love is something you can count on.

Dear God, when tough things happen,
remind me that you can still be relied on.

Praise

I will praise the LORD at all times;
his praise is always on my lips.
My whole being praises the LORD.

PSALM 34:1-2 NCV

Don't you love it when people say good things about you? God does too. Tell him right now some of the things you love about him. He is powerful, perfect, generous, merciful, loving, just, honest, and fair.

You can praise God with your words and by using your gifts to bring him glory. Use everything you've got to praise him. He loves to see what you give him and how you use the gifts he gave you to praise him.

Dear God, show me how to use my whole being to praise you.

Prayer Is Powerful

The prayer of a righteous person is powerful and effective.

JAMES 5:16 NIV

Do you make smoothies at home in a blender? By themselves, the smoothie ingredients taste good, but with the power of the blender, they change into something delicious!

When you pray, things happen. Prayer changes situations. Prayer changes people. Prayer is powerful and effective. You need to do your part and live a good life, and then God can use his power to make things happen.

Dear God, you are powerful. When I pray you make things happen. Thank you.

NOVEMBER 13

Whatever you do, whether in word or deed, do it all in the name of the Lord Jesus, giving thanks to God the Father through him.

COLOSSIANS 3:17 NIV

Anything you do can be a beautiful act of worship to God. Pick up your toys, give your parents a hug goodnight, or make a card for someone.

You don't have to be perfect. God is not disappointed when you make a mistake. He loves to see you trying and doing things out of joy because you love him. Just try your best. Think of something you could do today to show your love to God.

Dear God, you deserve the best.
I want to show my love for you each day.

Life Purpose

"It was not because of his sins or his parents' sins," Jesus answered. "This happened so the power of God could be seen in him."

JOHN 9:3 NLT

The disciples asked Jesus why a man was born blind. He couldn't see flowers or sunsets. He had never seen his mom or dad. He couldn't see the clothes he wore each day. He wished he could see. He wanted to have some kind of purpose. After Jesus healed him, he was so excited. His life was filled with purpose to give God glory.

That's the same purpose God gives you. Your purpose will always be to do whatever you do in a way that honors God and brings him glory.

Dear Jesus, thank you that you still heal people today. Show me your power and purpose for my life.

Worry Wars

"Can any one of you by worrying add a single hour to your life?"

MATTHEW 6:27 NIV

Some people worry way too much. Worrying doesn't make anything better; it just makes you feel worse, so why worry?

You can't control everything that happens, but you can control what's going on in your mind.

The more you think about God and good things, the less time you have to worry about other things. That's a good way to fight against worry.

Dear God, help me to focus on you and what's good.

NOVEMBER 16

Real Friends

There are "friends" who destroy each other,
but a real friend sticks closer than a brother.

ROMANS 15:13 NLT

God gave you such a special gift when he gave you friends. His plan is that you and your friends bring each other hope, joy, and peace. Unhealthy friendships do the opposite. They make you feel pressured to do things you don't want to do or confused about what is right and wrong. You don't want friends who leave you feeling like that.

A real friend builds up your confidence by encouraging you and supporting you. Talking with a real friend fills you up with hope and happiness.

Dear God, help me choose real friends who are good like you. Help me be a real friend too.

You Are Enough

God gave that grace to us freely, in Christ, the One he loves.

EPHESIANS 1:6 NCV

When you work hard, you want people to notice. Maybe you try to do something special or important so someone will notice you. It's good to work hard, but even if no one else says a thing, God notices.

God says that you are enough because he loves you. You matter to him. Nothing can separate you from God's forever love. God says you are enough just by being you.

Dear God, thank you that I matter to you.
I am enough to you.

Beauty that Lasts

Beauty does not last;
but a woman who fears the Lord
will be greatly praised.
Proverbs 31:30 NLT

After a lot of use, clothes wear out. You get holes in the knees of your jeans, rips and tears, and buttons pop off. Clothes don't last forever, and neither does beauty.

God makes each person beautiful in his own way. You might have a beautiful smile or lots of curly brown hair or a cute dimple in your cheek. Sadly, that kind of beauty will someday fade away. But if you become a Godly woman who respects the Lord, that is the kind of beauty that lasts.

Dear God, I want to look beautiful to you and have your kind of beauty that lasts forever.

Plan or Worry

Good planning and hard work lead to prosperity,
but hasty shortcuts lead to poverty.

PROVERBS 21:5 NLT

Worrying is not a good feeling. It makes your stomach hurt, and negative thoughts run around in your mind keeping you awake at night. Planning ahead can help you avoid worrying. Shortcuts will cause you a lot of stress.

Instead of worrying about what you didn't do or what has to be done, take control of the situation and your mind by making a plan.

Dear God, help me learn to plan ahead.
I don't want to worry about things I could avoid.

Vine and Branches

"I am the vine; you are the branches. If you remain in me and I in you, you will bear much fruit; apart from me you can do nothing."

JOHN 15:5 NIV

Jesus said if you stay close to him, he will make you grow and become all that he created you to be. If you pull a plant out of the ground, it will start to droop and dry up. If you pull away from God, the same will happen to you.

Read and listen to God's Word, stay grounded in his truth, and you will start to sprout and grow. Jesus is a wonderful gardener, and he invites you to join the growing process.

Dear Jesus, I want to stay close to you. Thank you for providing everything I need to grow.

Opening a Gift

Sing joyfully to the Lord.
Sing to him a new song;
play skillfully, and shout for joy.

Psalm 33:1, 3 NIV

The verses in the Bible are like a gift. God packs each one with treasures for you to discover. These verses talk about singing a new song to the Lord. He loves it when you are creative.

Play skillfully for God by practicing and doing your best for him. Shout for joy with confidence and be bold in how you worship. Don't worry about who is watching you. Dig into the verses in the Bible like you are opening a gift that God gave you.

Dear Lord Jesus, thank you for the gift of your words in the Bible.

Small Beginnings

"Do not despise these small beginnings, for the LORD rejoices to see the work begin."

ZECHARIAH 4:10 NLT

Most things start small. You may have a big idea, but there are steps you need to take before it can happen. You may need to start out small by volunteering or watching someone else do the thing you are interested in. Then you can step up and help do it with them until finally you are able to do it all on your own.

Big things start with little things. Keep practicing and doing a good job where you are. God sees you trying, and he is proud of all the work you do.

Dear God, sometimes the small stuff doesn't seem important. Help me to do my best all the time.

NOVEMBER 23

What Pleases God

Live as children of light and find out what pleases the Lord.

EPHESIANS 5:8, 10 NIV

Do you have a favorite teacher or coach? You probably like to please them, love to help whenever they ask, and you work hard for them. When you like someone, making that person happy doesn't feel like work.

The same is true with God. The verse above says to find out what pleases the Lord. When you love the Lord, you also want to make him proud of you. Look for ways you can please God today.

Dear God, teach me what pleases you.
I like to make you happy.

Now and Then

Our homeland is in heaven, and we are waiting for our Savior, the Lord Jesus Christ, to come from heaven.

PHILIPPIANS 3:20 NCV

When you put your faith in Jesus, your forever home will be in heaven. All the stuff you have now will not be needed there. Toys, phones, computers, TVs, and bikes are just for now. They are fun and useful, but they won't last forever, and you won't need them in heaven with God.

It's ok to have stuff for now but remember the important things that last forever.

Dear Jesus, I appreciate everything you've given me. Help me to remember that my forever home is in heaven.

Seasoned with Salt

Let your conversation be always full of grace, seasoned with salt, so that you may know how to answer everyone.

COLOSSIANS 4:6 NIV

Salt makes things taste better. You don't need a lot. A sprinkle will do. It adds more flavor to food, and it also helps make some foods last longer.

How do you let your conversation be full of grace and seasoned with salt? Notice how the person you are talking to is responding. Choose words that make them feel better. Speak with kindness, love, and truth. Think about the words you say today. Are they sprinkled with grace?

Dear Lord, help me think carefully about the words I choose to say.

NOVEMBER 26

Word Food

From the fruit of their mouth a person's stomach is filled;
with the harvest of their lips they are satisfied.

PROVERBS 18:20 NIV

If your words were food, how would they taste? Do you say hurtful things that make others feel bad, or do your words add sweetness to other people's lives? Angry words can burn like a spicy pepper and make people cry. Encouraging words can be like fruit, full of vitamins that make you stronger.

Think about your conversations like a meal. Do people walk away from talking to you and feel full or empty?

Dear God, remind me to think of what I say
and how I say it.

NOVEMBER 27

Loyalty

Elisha said, "As surely as the LORD lives and as you yourself live, I will not leave you."

2 KINGS 2:2 NIV

Best friends are great to have for fun times like sleepovers and parties. Best friends are also great for bad days and sad news. The best friends to have are loyal. They will stick up for you when no one else does, and they will be there for you when you need someone to comfort you.

How do you think your friends would describe you? Would they say you are a loyal friend? Who can you be a loyal friend to?

Dear God, I need friends who stick up for me. Help me be a loyal friend to them as well.

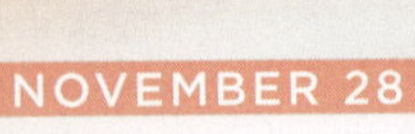

Causing Trouble

"Just as stirring milk makes butter,
and twisting noses makes them bleed,
so stirring up anger causes trouble."

PROVERBS 30:33 NCV

Actions have consequences. The good news is that you can help avoid bad consequences by changing your actions. Choose a better action and you will probably get a better reaction. Instead of yelling back at your brother, try to be calm when you talk. Instead of talking back, listen to what your mom is saying.

Is there someone you argue with a lot? How can you change what you say to get a better result?

Dear God, help me make better choices
in how I respond to people.

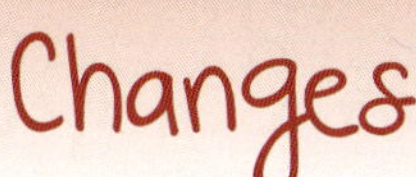

Changes

There is a time for everything,
and everything on earth has its special season.

ECCLESIASTES 3:1 NCV

Every fall the leaves turn from deep green to bright orange, ruby red, and golden yellow. The change in season from summer to fall means splashes of color that will eventually fall to the ground as winter comes.

Changing seasons is a normal and good process for nature. People change too. You keep growing taller. You change on the inside as well. Even your thinking is changing. All these changes are normal and good. God has a good plan for all these changes.

Dear God, thank you for the good and normal changes that are part of your plan for me.

Gracious Compliments

Let someone else praise you,
and not your own mouth;
an outsider, and not your own lips.

PROVERBS 27:2 NIV

Getting a compliment can feel funny. You might be embarrassed with the attention and want to hide away. It's hard to know how to respond to someone telling you how wonderful they think you are. Other people love getting compliments. They feel seen, noticed, admired.

Praise, like a compliment, is a gift. It is something you are given, not something you take, so don't compliment yourself. The best way to handle a compliment is to just say thank you and smile.

Dear God, thank you for people who choose to encourage me by giving compliments.

DECEMBER
“The LORD himself will go ahead of you.
He will be with you.
He will never leave you.
He’ll never desert you.
So don’t be afraid.
Don’t lose hope.”
DEUTERONOMY 31:8 NIRV

Overflowing Hope

May the God of hope fill you with all joy and peace as you trust in him, so that you may overflow with hope by the power of the Holy Spirit.

ROMANS 15:13 NIV

The weeks leading up to Christmas are a time to prepare your heart and remember Jesus coming to earth as a baby. The Israelites waited for many years in hope of a Savior. Jesus came with hope that overflowed to those around him.

Jesus is coming back again, and when he does, we will all be together in heaven where there will only be good things! That is a wonderful kind of hope.

Dear God, thank you for giving me hope that good things are ahead.

The Best Gift

"Today your Savior was born in the town of David.
He is Christ, the Lord."

LUKE 2:11 NCV

It is nice to sit by the Christmas tree and enjoy the twinkling lights. It is exciting to think about opening the gifts and getting to enjoy what's inside. Maybe you have been waiting a long time for a special gift that you really want.

Gifts are a fun part of Christmas, but the best gift isn't found under your Christmas tree. It's inside your heart. Jesus came to earth as a baby so you could have forgiveness and eternal life. That gift is too big to fit in a box.

Dear Jesus, thank you for coming to show me how to live. I accept your gift of salvation.

Shaped

Do not be shaped by this world; instead be changed within by a new way of thinking.

ROMANS 12:2 NCV

There are people and things all around you trying to shape how you think and what you do. Movies, TV, social media, school, even your friends and family are all giving you advice on what you should think and buy and what's important in life.

Whatever you listen to will shape how you think and the choices you make, so be sure your life is being shaped by God's Word.

Dear God, help me not to be influenced by what other people think. I want to please you.

Choosing Joy

"I will give you hidden treasures,
riches stored in secret places,
so that you may know that I am the LORD,
the God of Israel, who summons you by name."

ISAIAH 45:3 NIV

Do know someone who is in a lot of pain every day? That is called suffering. It can be difficult to be happy and choose to have joy in your heart when you are suffering. Pain can make a person grumpy.

For those who follow Jesus, there is a reward in heaven. God said he has hidden treasures and riches stored in secret places. When bad things happen, remember that God can uncover sweet treasures of joy in the middle of hard times.

Dear God, help me to choose joy even in hard times.

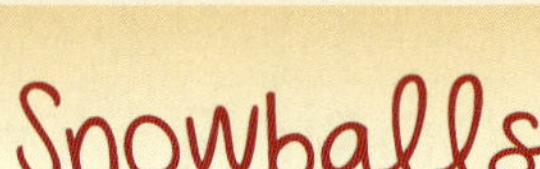

Snowballs

Fix your thoughts on what is true, and honorable, and right, and pure, and lovely, and admirable. Think about things that are excellent and worthy of praise.

PHILIPPIANS 4:8 NLT

Every snowman starts as a small snowball. Pack cold, wet snow into a ball, then roll it around in more snow until the ball grows bigger and bigger. Pretty soon you've got a really big snowball.

Thoughts are like a snowball that starts small and grows bigger. One negative thought gets rolling, and it's hard to stop. That is why this verse tells you to take control of your thoughts and think about things that are good and worthy of praise.

Dear God, help me take control of negative thoughts and think about things that are true, right, and good instead.

Jingle Bells

The grass dries up. The flowers fall to the ground.
But what our God says will stand forever.

Isaiah 40:8 NIrV

The Christmas song "Jingle Bells" has been around for a long time. Children in Massachusetts started singing this song in 1850 and it has lasted over a hundred and sixty years.

The words in the Bible have been around much longer. God's Word will last forever. Because God never changes, his Word will never change either. You can be sure that it is still true today, and it will last forever.

Dear God, thank you for your Word and all the pages full of your power and love.

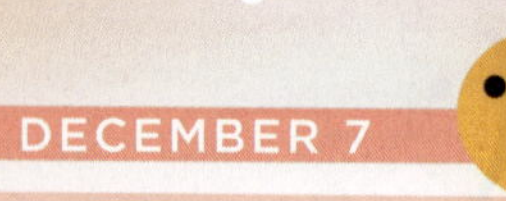

A Birth Announcement

To us a child is born, to us a son is given.
And he will be called Wonderful Counselor, Mighty God,
Everlasting Father, Prince of Peace.

ISAIAH 9:6 NIV

Parents are so excited to announce when their new baby is born. A birth announcement will usually say the baby's full name and the date the baby was born.

When the angels made Jesus's birth announcement, they gave God the glory. One of Jesus' names is the Prince of Peace. Jesus gives you peace with God, peace with other people, and one day he will bring peace to the whole world.

Dear Jesus, please use me to bring your peace to the people I know.

Party

"There is joy in heaven over one sinner who turns away from sin."

LUKE 15:10 NIRV

Craft parties are fun for creative people. A pool party is fun if you love to swim. A tea party is a great opportunity to dress up. A pizza party is delicious. The kind of party you choose tells a lot about what you like.

God loves to welcome new believers into his family. Every time someone turns away from their sin and asks God to forgive them, God and the angels celebrate. Give God a reason to throw a party by telling people the good news.

Dear God, show me who I should share your good news with.

Knitting

I am certain that God, who began the good work within you, will continue his work until it is finally finished on the day when Christ Jesus returns.

PHILIPPIANS 1:6 NLT

Some people knit scarves or crochet stuffed animals for fundraisers. When they begin with a ball of yarn it's hard to tell what they are making. It takes a while for the rows of yarn to take shape.

God is working at making those who believe in Jesus into something beautiful. He has started a good work in you. You are not finished, but you are on the way!

Dear God, help me to remember that you are working in everyone including me.

DECEMBER 10

Little Lambs

He gathers the lambs in his arms
and carries them close to his heart;
he gently leads those that have young.

Isaiah 40:11 NIV

Woolly little lambs are so cute, and their tiny bleat for their mama is even cuter. Those cute little lambs are curious, and they can also get into a lot of trouble. They jump fences looking for better grass to eat. They follow other sheep into dangerous situations. They wander off and get lost. They need a shepherd to watch over them.

People sometimes act like sheep. Jesus is called the Good Shepherd because he goes to rescue the person who is lost and far away from his protection. He loves you and everyone else.

Dear Jesus, thank you for loving me so much even when I wander away and do my own thing.

DECEMBER 11

Offended

Search me, God, and know my heart;
test me and know my anxious thoughts.
See if there is any offensive way in me,
and lead me in the way everlasting.

PSALM 139:23-24 NIV

If you spend enough time with someone, there will be a chance for them to do something that hurts your feelings. When it's a big deal, you can sometimes call it being offended. It's like being hurt and mad at the same time. Just like you have feelings that get hurt, so does God. Doing what you know is wrong hurts and offends God.

Take a minute to ask God if there's anything in your life that makes his heart sad. Ask God to lead you and help you make wise choices that lead to everlasting life with him.

Dear God, I know I'm supposed to do what's right.
Help me to choose the everlasting way.

Presentable

God shows his great love for us in this way: Christ died for us while we were still sinners.

Romans 5:8 NCV

You want to look your best when you are going to a special event. You will wear your best clothes, your best shoes. Your hair will be fixed pretty, your teeth brushed, and fingernails clean. You want to be presentable and make a good impression on the people at the special event.

You don't need to make yourself presentable before you come to Jesus. You don't need to try to be better before asking him for forgiveness.

Dear God, thank you for loving me just as I am.

DECEMBER 13

"The Lord bless you and keep you;
the Lord make his face shine on you and be gracious to you;
the Lord turn his face toward you and give you peace."

Numbers 6:24-26 niv

God told Moses to have the priest speak this blessing over his people. God wanted his people to know that he was for them, not against them. His blessing is for you too.

If no one has ever spoken this blessing over you, that's okay. You can read this blessing out loud to yourself right now.

Dear God, thank you for your blessing.

Gift Giving

"Even though you are evil, you know how to give good gifts to your children. How much more will your Father who is in heaven give good gifts to those who ask him!"

Matthew 7:11 NIRV

If you walked in the door for lunch and asked for a PB&J sandwich, would your mom hand you a rock to eat? Or if you asked your grandma for a snack, would she hand you a snake instead? Of course they wouldn't do that, but that's how some people picture God. They are afraid that if they ask him for something, he'll give them something they don't want instead. That's not what God is like at all.

God knows how to give good gifts. When you ask God for something, you can expect he will give you just what you need.

Dear God, you are a good Father who gives good gifts. Thank you.

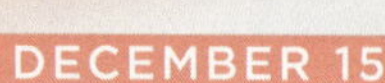

Those who hope in the LORD
will renew their strength.
They will soar on wings like eagles;
they will run and not grow weary,
they will walk and not be faint.

ISAIAH 40:31 NIV

What gift do you hope you will get for Christmas? That hope is like a sparkle of excitement inside you. Hope is believing that something good can happen.

What happens when what you hope for doesn't turn out? People change, things change, life changes. Remember, God is the most reliable person in your life. You will never be disappointed when your hope is in him.

Dear God, I choose to put my hope in you.

Giving Gifts

God is so rich in mercy, and he loved us so much, that even though we were dead because of our sins, he gave us life when he raised Christ from the dead.

EPHESIANS 2:4-5 NLT

Giving gifts is what you do at Christmas because God gave the gift of his only Son, and Jesus gave the gift of his life. Those are pretty special gifts.

God loved the world and all the people in it so much that he made it possible for everyone who believes in him to have eternal life. When you confess your sins and believe in Jesus, God gives you this gift, so you can live with him in heaven forever.

Dear God, I love getting gifts at Christmas, but I love your gift of new life even more.

Promise Keeper

Every word of God can be trusted.

PROVERBS 30:5 ICB

If someone makes a promise, you know they will do what they say if you can trust them. You know who is and who isn't a good promise keeper by what they have said and done in the past.

The more you get to know God, the more you will see that he always keeps his promises. He is faithful, honest, and trustworthy. If you're having trouble trusting God, spend a little time getting to know him by reading his Word and talking to him.

Dear God, I believe you keep your promises. I want to know you more, so my faith will grow stronger.

Say No

It teaches us not to live against God nor to do the evil things the world wants to do. Instead, that grace teaches us to live in the present age in a wise and right way and in a way that shows we serve God.

TITUS 2:12 NCV

There are two ways to live your life. You can live against God and do the evil things the world wants you to do, or you can live the right way that pleases God. When you're tempted to lie about what really happened, or take something that's not yours, say no.

You know the right way to live. You know what a good choice is. Walk in those good ways that show you love and serve God.

Dear God, give me the courage and strength to say no to what's wrong and yes to what is right.

Most Important

We set our eyes not on what we see but on what we cannot see. What we see will last only a short time, but what we cannot see will last forever.

2 Corinthians 4:18 NCV

What are the things that matter most? What things couldn't you live without? It's the things that last. It's the things you don't see.

You don't see God or heaven, and it's hard to understand or imagine what eternity will look like, but that is what matters. Keep focused on God, who you cannot see, and think about what lasts forever. Whatever is most important to God should be most important to you.

Dear God, help me to remember what matters most is living for you.

Get It All Done

"Martha, Martha, you are worried and upset about many things. Only one thing is important. Mary has chosen the better thing, and it will never be taken away from her."

LUKE 10:41-42 NCV

Company was coming and Martha was trying to get ready. Her sister Mary wasn't helping at all. Instead, she was sitting by Jesus, listening to his every word like there was nothing else to do. Martha was upset that she had to do all the work while Mary sat.

Jesus said that Mary chose the better thing, which was spending time with him. Life gets busy, and it's easy to push your time with God to the side. Be like Mary and choose the better thing.

Dear God, help me take time to listen to your words.

Pretty Packages

When troubles of any kind come your way, consider it an opportunity for great joy. For you know that when your faith is tested, your endurance has a chance to grow.

JAMES 1:2-3 NLT

Some gifts don't come wrapped in pretty packages. You can give the gift of serving and pull weeds in your grandma's garden. You can give the gift of friendship and invite a new neighbor to play at your house.

Change how you think of a problem. You will have more joy when you see things in a positive way. What might look like trouble could become an opportunity for great joy.

Dear God, help me to see the good possibilities in a problem. Thank you for your great joy.

Joy to the World

Everyone on earth is amazed
at the wonderful things you have done.
What you do makes people
from one end of the earth to the other
sing for joy.

PSALM 65:8 NIRV

Listen to the song *Joy to the World*. It is one of the most well-known Christmas songs and shouts about joy for the whole world because Jesus has come. Jesus is the focus of the Christmas season, not the presents or decorations or cookies and treats.

When God created the world, he said that each thing was good. Then sin entered the world and sadness, death, and pain grew. Jesus rules with truth and grace, so you don't have to fear. You can be filled with joy and wonder because of his great love.

Dear God, thank you for the wonderful things you have done.

Cinnamon Rolls

"Do you give me orders about the work of my hands?
I am the one who made the earth
and created people to live on it.
With my hands I stretched out the heavens."

ISAIAH 45:11-12 NLT

Christmas is a time of family traditions. Cinnamon rolls are a favorite Christmas treat for many families. They are big and fluffy, filled with cinnamon and sugar, and glazed with delicious frosting. Family recipes are usually passed down by someone who knows what they are doing.

God knows what he's doing in your life, your family, your school, and your city. He is in control. He never makes mistakes. You can relax and trust him to work things out for good.

Dear God, I trust you. Some things don't make sense, but I know that you are in control.

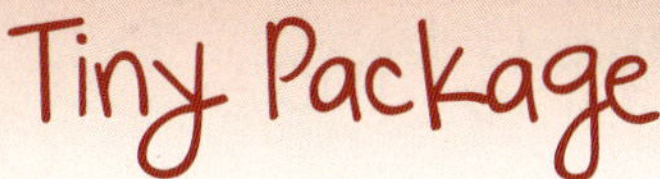

Tiny Package

Never let loyalty and kindness leave you!
Tie them around your neck as a reminder.
Write them deep within your heart.

PROVERBS 3:3 NLT

Some gifts are big, and some are small. Some people put a lot of effort into wrapping gifts, and some just use a gift bag. The gift you get might not look special, but what if that tiny package holds a pretty necklace?

Loyalty and kindness are like a necklace that God tells you to wear. Never take them off; wear them wherever you go. You want to be known as someone who is caring and trustworthy.

Dear God, I want to be kind and loyal because that is what you want me to be.

Christmas Day

There were shepherds living out in the fields nearby, keeping watch over their flocks at night. An angel of the Lord appeared to them, and the glory of the Lord shone around them, and they were terrified. But the angel said to them, "Do not be afraid. I bring you good news that will cause great joy for all the people."

LUKE 2:8-10 NIV

It's Christmas Day! How exciting! Christmas is the time of year that you remember the exciting, good news that the Savior of the world has come. That is worth celebrating and definitely causes great joy.

Sing songs like the choir of angels sang to the shepherds. Read the Christmas story from the Bible. Remind yourself that Jesus is the greatest gift. However you celebrate on Christmas Day, do it with a heart full of joy

Dear God, I am so excited for the good news!

Christmas Music

"Give glory to God in heaven,
and on earth let there be peace
to the people who please God."

LUKE 2:13-14 ICB

Christmas music is fun to sing. What are some of your favorite Christmas songs? Leading up to Christmas you will hear it wherever you go: in the car, in stores, at restaurants, and at church.

This verse talks about a heavenly army of angels praising God. That would be so amazing to see and hear. Christmas music is fun, and some songs are funny, but it is also a chance to worship God. Give praise and glory to him today!

Dear Jesus, thank you for the gift of music.
When I sing, I want to use my voice to give you glory.

Home in Your Heart

Christ will make his home in your hearts as you trust in him. Your roots will grow down into God's love and keep you strong.

EPHESIANS 3:17 NLT

Imagine your body is a tree. Your toes are the roots growing down into the soil, and your arms are the strong branches. Now picture your heart as a hole in the middle of the tree trunk and God's love sits inside like a wise owl. Isn't that a fun picture of God making his home in your heart?

If Jesus lives in your heart, then his love will pour out of you. People will notice when Jesus is in your heart.

Dear Jesus, thank you for coming into my heart and filling me with your love.

Prince of Peace

"Peace I leave with you; my peace I give you. I do not give to you as the world gives. Do not let your hearts be troubled and do not be afraid."

JOHN 14:27 NIV

Peace is something everyone needs. It doesn't feel good to be restless, anxious, worried, or afraid. One way people feel God's presence is when calm settles in their hearts. It is a wonderful feeling.

Imagine a baby crying, and then the father walks into the room, gently picks her up, wraps his loving arms around her, rocks back and forth, and shushes the baby into a peaceful sleep. That is how it feels to have the peace that Jesus offers.

Dear Jesus, thank you for giving me peace.

DECEMBER 29

Plans for You

"I know the plans I have for you," declares the LORD, "plans to prosper you and not to harm you, plans to give you hope and a future."

JEREMIAH 29:11 NIV

It is good to know that God is in control. He has had plans for you before you were born. And they are good plans.

The New Year is coming. It is a time when you can look back on all the good things God did for you and look forward to more of his goodness in the next year. What are some things you hope will happen? Pray about it. Set some goals and ask God what he wants for you.

Dear Lord Jesus, thank you that you have good plans for my life.

DECEMBER 30

For Ever and Ever

This God is our God for ever and ever;
he will be our guide even to the end.

PSALM 48:14 NIV

As you come to the end of the year, look back and try to see Jesus in your memories. Praise God for all the prayers he answered. Some moments in the year would have been happy, and some were sad, but God was there for all of them.

The God you serve is powerful and amazing. He has been God for ever and ever. Before the world existed, God was there. He knows everything. He has seen everything. You can trust and follow him. There is no one like him.

Dear God, you are amazing. Please keep guiding me throughout my whole life.

A New Thing

"I am doing a new thing!
Now it springs up; do you not perceive it?
I am making a way in the wilderness."

ISAIAH 43:18-19 NIV

It's countdown to midnight and to a new year. New Year's resolutions are something people do all around the world. This means they decide to make good, healthy changes in their lives.

God said that he was doing a new thing. He was making a way for us to come to him through Jesus. The year ahead is full of chances for you to follow in Jesus' footsteps and make better choices. Ask God what he wants you to change and start a new thing!

Dear God, thank you for a new year and a fresh start. Thank you for doing a new thing and making a way for me to have life through Jesus.